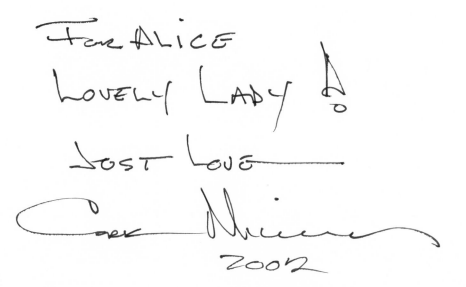

For ALICE
LOVELY LADY
JUST LOVE

2002

PORTRAITS

Nonfiction Books by Cork Millner
Vintage Valley
Sherry—The Golden Wine of Spain
Wines and Wineries of Santa Barbara
Recipes by the Winemakers
Santa Barbara Celebrities—Conversations from the American Riviera
The Art of Interviewing
Write from the Start
Polo—The King of Sports
Portraits

Coauthored with Lynda Millner
Looking Great *Without* Diet or Exercise

Coauthored with Hara
Flamingo! A Photographer's Odyssey

Coauthored with Cass Warner Sperling
Hollywood Be Thy Name—The Warner Brothers Story

Portraits

by Cork Millner

DRAWINGS BY
Barnaby Conrad

Fithian Press

SANTA BARBARA • 1994

FIRST EDITION

Design and typography by Jim Cook

Published by Fithian Press
A division of Daniel & Daniel, Publishers, Inc.
Post Office Box 1525 • Santa Barbara, California 93101

LIBRARY OF CONGRESS CATALOGING-IN-PUBLICATION DATA
    Millner, Cork
    Portraits, creative conversations with celebrities / Cork Millner
        p. cm.
    ISBN 1-56474-087-0
    1. Celebrities—Interviews. 2. United States—Biography.
    3. Biography—20th century. I. Title.
    CT220.M55 1994
    920.073—dc20   93-45820
                                                   CIP

To Lynda
—Cork Millner

To Mary
—Barnaby Conrad

"I didn't think I was that nice.
But then, you writers can do miracles."
—KARL MALDEN

Portraits

| Introduction | *Creating the Portrait* | 11 |

Hollywood Be Thy Name

Robert Mitchum	*The Mitchum Style*	19
Ruby Keeler	*42nd Street Baby*	31
James Stewart	*Ah . . . Waal . . . It's Jimmy Stewart*	41
Ronald Reagan	*The Errol Flynn of the "B's"*	55
Jane Russell	*Gentlemen Prefer Brunettes*	67
Rod Steiger	*Running Hot and Cold*	77
Jane Seymour	*Miracle Woman*	87
Bo Derek	*Home On the Range*	97
John Travolta	*Look Who's Talking, Too*	109
Ann Jillian	*Through the Looking Glass*	119
Sharon Stone	*Stone Goddess*	129
Chris Mitchum	*My Father's Footsteps*	137

It Was a Dark and Stormy Night

Charles Schulz	*Working for Peanuts*	147
Cathy Guisewite	*Cathy!*	159
Jackie Collins	*Hollywood's Literary Lioness*	169

The Comedy Store

Jonathan Winters	*A Season of Winters*	179
Steve Allen	*Hi-Ho, Steverino!*	191
Steve Martin	*A Wild and Serious Guy*	199

Happy Hollandaise

| Julia Child | *Inside Julia's Kitchen* | 207 |

Blood and Sand

| John Fulton | *An American Matador in Spain* | 217 |

Introduction
Creating the Portrait

When Robert Mitchum first looked at the portrait that Barnaby Conrad had rendered, he joked, "You sure made me look like a mean son of a bitch." Conrad pointed a finger skyward. "No, Robert, I didn't," he said affably. "God did."

CREATING a life-like portrait of a famous personality, either from a drawing or during a one-on-one interview session, can be a challenging, sometimes whimsical, often intense, even embarrassing adventure. It's like going on a blind date—and ending up married. The author and the subject try to make a good impression on one another, not sure if the "date" will turn into a pleasant interlude or a why-did-I-agree-to-get-myself-into-this escapade.

Witness the following:

When I rang the doorbell to Dame Judith Anderson's home, I was greeted by a chorus of barking. Dame Judith, the diminutive dramatic actress knighted by Elizabeth II, opened the door.

Between her legs were two dachshunds, yapping away.

Dame Judith looked down and intoned, "Shhusssh!" which in dachshund language means bark louder. Then, in a deep voice that rang with

11

the resonance and electricity that poet Robinson Jeffers once referred to as "liquid fire," Dame Judith said, "Oh, do come in."

I walked across the threshold—and stepped into dog doo.

An equally embarrassing moment?

At actress Eva Marie Saint's home I was met by her producer/director husband, Jeffery Hayden, who said Eva Marie was dressing, and asked if I would like something to drink.

Yes, coffee.

Moments later, he returned from the kitchen with a steaming cup, and at the same time Eva Marie glided in from the bedroom. Hayden thrust the cup at me; Eva Marie her hand. I reached for both, dropped the notebook from under my arm, grabbed for the cup and the actress's hand—and spilled the coffee over the front of my light tan pants.

Stunned silence.

Finally, we sat down for the interview and as the question/answer session unfolded, my pants began to dry—and the dark stain slowly vanished. They kept glancing at my pants, a disconcerting feeling for an interviewer. By the end of the session, the pants had dried, and the stain was gone. As I rose, Hayden asked, "Where did you buy those pants?"

Challenging moments?

Jimmy Stewart is a legend. As such, he has been interviewed countless times, and has answered every question. As the interview progressed in the comfort of the actor's living room, I kept hearing the same responses I had unearthed in my research. How to get something new? Then, on the coffee table between us, I noticed a filigree statuette of a standing rabbit, complete with top hat and black bow tie. Recalling that Stewart had played Elwood P. Dowd in *Harvey*, I asked if there was a chance I could speak with Harvey before I left.

Stewart's eyes glinted. "Ah . . . waal . . . Harvey's upstairs taking a nap."

Perhaps I could chat with him after he wakes up?

"Ah . . . you see, Harvey doesn't talk much until he's had his first cup of coffee."

Introduction

Intense moments?

When Rod Steiger met me at the door of his Malibu home, he glared at me, thrust out his hand, and growled, "I'm Rod Steiger!" The intensity of that moment carried us through the next hour-and-a-half, as each question I asked was met by a nose-to-nose response that made me feel as if I were in front of the cameras involved in a dramatic scene. Such as the moment he described a scene in which he became so intense it frightened him:

"And I went on for thirty more seconds improvising until at the end I was screaming with hostility. We cut and there was dead silence on the set. I realized it showed something sick in me, this maniac inside of me came out."

Steiger's eyes ignited as he thrust his face a few inches from mine and hissed: "And—it—scared—me—to—death!"

Whimsical moments?

When I walked into Jonathan Winters's tiny studio where he creates his surrealistic paintings, I discovered the comedian in a hard-backed chair in the corner, dressed in a Cincinnati Reds baseball uniform, sitting stiffly as a cigar store dummy. For what seemed like an eternity he didn't move or crack a smile. Finally I said, "Hello, how are you?" a question that spawned a two-hour performance from the improvisational comedy master. I hardly said another word. As Winters led me to the door, he grinned sardonically, "You sure ask great questions."

Another whimsical moment from a comedian?

I saw Steve Martin sitting at a table in a Santa Barbara courtyard. I slipped behind a purple bougainvillea—feeling as ridiculous as Inspector Clouseau—and watched as he sipped from a cup of coffee. Stepping from behind the bush, I walked to Martin's table.

"Uh . . . I'm a writer, and I . . . ah . . . " The next words tumbled from my mouth without benefit of passing through my brain: "Uh . . . do you know where I can find Jonathan Winters?"

The comedian's head swiveled slowly toward me like a macabre scene from *The Exorcist*, and he said, "That's almost funny."

Uh-oh moments?

I arrived at Anne Francis's home ten minutes early and parked just down the street. At the appointed interview time, I drove into the circular drive of her home. The actress, a light breeze fanning her long blond hair, opened the front door and called, "You're on time!"

I replied, "I'm always on time."

She smiled. "I know. I saw your car parked down there ten minutes ago!"

Rewarding moments?

Moments like listening to Ronald Reagan as he recounted the good old days when he made forty-three movies for Warner Brothers, and how hard he had worked to shuck the mold of a "B" actor and make great films, such as his two favorites, *King's Row* and *Knute Rockne—All American,* in which he played one of his favorite roles as the Gipper.

The reward came after the interview when I heard one of his cadre of secretaries say, "It was great hearing him having fun in an interview, laughing, telling stories."

Surprising moments?

Julia Child responding to my phone call query by saying, "Oh, do drop by for lunch," only to arrive and discover that all her ovens were inoperative.

Happily, she served cold quail from the refrigerator, with all those creamy sauces.

Tongue-in-cheek moments:

Bo Derek, responding to my question, "Does John ever get mad at you, and if so, what does he do?" by saying with an impish grin: "Oh, he says he'll go down to the high school and find a younger one."

Touching moments:

Cartoonist Cathy Guisewite calling thirty minutes after I had delivered her profile, and in a tearful Cathy-from-the-comic-strip voice, saying, "Thank you for making me sound so coherent."

Wonderful one-liners:

Jimmy Stewart's response to the question, "Have you ever thought of running for government office?" came slowly: "Ah . . . waal . . . I don't talk fast enough to be a politician."

Robert Mitchum's disgruntled reply when asked what he did for exercise was: "I breathe in, I breathe out."

Don Murray's quick answer to, "Of all the famous personalities in world history, who would you like most to have lunch with?" was "Jesus."

I asked broadcast journalist Ralph Story if he agreed with Gay Talese, who once said, "Most journalists are restless voyeurs who see warts on the world . . . Gloom is their game, the spectacle their passion, normality their nemesis."

After a thoughtful moment, Story replied, "I think he's right—to a degree. You have to remember that it's a reporter's job to find those warts, to prod and probe, to get in the way, to be curious, to be annoying, even vicious . . . We're really not persecuting; it's just our business to pry."

Like Goya laying bare the degeneration of Carlos IV and the Spanish royal family, it is the task of the portrait artist and the profile author to pry, to chip away at the smiling public façade of today's celebrities and reveal the true nature of the personality.

The result is a life-like portrait.

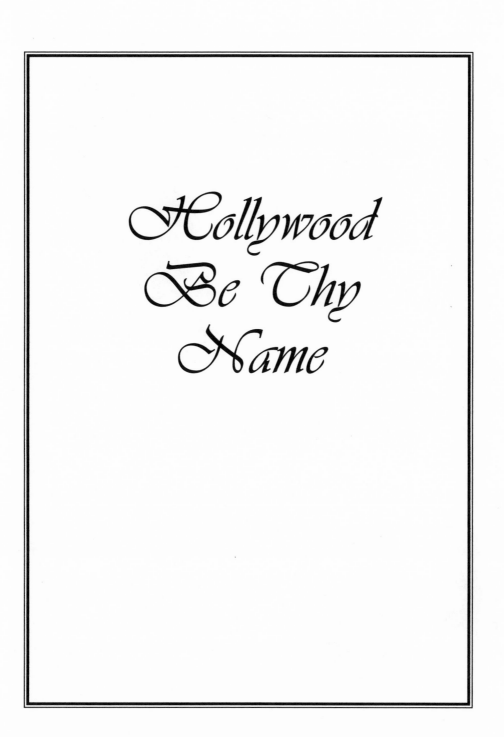

Hollywood
Be Thy
Name

Barnaby Conrad
1986

Robert Mitchum
The Mitchum Style

"Exercise? I breathe in, I breathe out."

MITCHUM. Alone. Sitting in a flowered sofa chair, a shot of tequila and a wedge of lime in one fist, a plate of kidney pie tottering on his knees. He pays no attention to the bloody-mary-for-brunch crowd that swirls around him at the buffet party.

He glances distastefully at the plate of kidney pie, then jams a hand inside the pocket of his sport coat, pulls out an unfiltered cigarette, stuffs it between his lips, and in a rich voice begins to talk—about Mitchum and the movies.

"On the screen I've played everything except midgets and women. No, wait, I can remember one of the first pictures I worked on—what the hell was its name, yeah, *The Girl Rush* for RKO in 1944—I was in drag." He grins, the lines in his lived-in face deepening. "As a character actor I've done Chinese laundrymen, Irish washerwomen, faggots . . . Hell, you paint eyes on my eyelids, and I'll walk through any part."

The cigarette bobs up and down in the corner of his mouth—only

Bogart could do it better—as he adds, "I figure people come to see my films just so they can say, 'Is that old son of a bitch still around?'"

There is no aura of phony glamour, no puffed-up *amour-propre* as Mitchum talks about himself. "Whenever I run across an actor with an ego the size of the Chrysler building, I tell him the greatest movie star that ever lived was an old spayed hound named Rin Tin Tin," he says.

Perceived as a rebel, a Hollywood bad boy, Mitchum shrugs and says, "Hell, I don't know what a rebel is. Look, I come in ready for work, just like an old whore who's got nothing to get ready. It's like having a job. Like a plumber. Yeah, I'm a good plumber: I show up on time, bring all my tools—so I don't have to go back for a second trip—then say the jokes, punch out, and go home."

Mitchum *is* good at his craft. *Time* magazine described him as "one of the most respected professionals in the business, a no-nonsense actor who is never late on the set and knows his lines cold."

What does Mitchum think of his acting talent?

"I fill in the empty spaces, and they pay me for it. It's better than working. I'm for hire in pictures"—he calls them "pictures" as if he is attempting to downgrade them—"at a certain fee. If they can get someone for less, then get him. The way I look at it, I must be pretty good at what I do: for what other reason would they have hauled me around the world in *The Winds of War*?" (He received approximately $1 million for making that 1983 miniseries.)

"Winds of War!" Mitchum continues, his voice rumbling like a volcano about to erupt. "Hell, on that one I spent fifteen months filming it and it damn near killed me! We were shooting in Zagreb, Yugoslavia and I had a temperature of 104 degrees from some local strain of virus. I mean, people were dying of it! They sent me to this doctor, and I told him: 'Watch this!' coughed and sprayed blood all over the joint. He said: 'That's great! How did you do it? Movie special effects?'"

Mitchum's growl shifts into a Viennese doctor's high-pitched whine (he can mimic any voice, use any accent) as he continues, "'You sweating? You have temperature? How long haf you been sveating?' I said,

'Ever since I got here.' He said, 'Yah, yah, that is very serious. Many germs goink around. You got it!'" Mitchum rolls his eyes. "Hell, he didn't even give me a shot."

Mitchum lifts the glass in a toast. "Well, the locals gave me a hell of a toast for the flu. It was called *grappa*—180 proof." He bites into the lime wedge then drinks the tequila down neat, head back, all in one silver-bullet gulp.

A maid comes by in a black-and-white uniform and eyes Mitchum's plate. He looks at her with that unique sleepy-lidded look of smoldering sensuality that has become his movie trademark, then stabs his cigarette into the kidney pie where it sizzles and sputters in the brown sauce. The maid quickly takes the plate away.

He sighs, satisfied. For a moment he had been "on," the consummate actor plying his trade, a star in his firmament.

"Nah, I was never a star, really. I just don't have the sense of popular identity that people have of me."

What about fame, then?

"I'm a popular freak."

And what does he think about his ability to stay at the top of the Hollywood heap for fifty years?

"I work cheap. I work fast. I don't waste a lot of time hyping myself up with method acting. Like Bruce Dern, who I worked with in *That Championship Season*—Dern's crazy! Sure, he's good; he just wants to be the world's middle-weight champion actor. You turn the camera on him and it takes him forty minutes to get ready. It's like Brando saying 'Hello' on camera. Hell, that takes him twenty minutes. In *That Championship Season* I played a basketball coach, and I finally had to tell the director I had never seen a basketball game. That went over like a fart in church."

That's vintage Mitchum. He loves to tell stories, from tiny ones to granddaddy whoppers. Each tale is used to divert the curious intruder, to make sure that the real Mitchum, the personal Mitchum, the *inner* Mitchum, is shaded from the searing view of the inquisitor. So, he plays the grouch, the grumbler, the brawler, the iconoclast, ready to smash any idol—including himself.

"I choose not to say why I act the way I do," he says with a shrug.

He is, by his own admission, a "lousy interview." His I-don't-give-a-damn aggressive, knock-down-drag-out style of responding to questions alienates most interviewers, and many times sullies his image in the public's view.

Mitchum lights another cigarette, inhales a satisfying drag. "In an interview I react by momentary instinct. I am bound to say something that will piss somebody off. Sometimes I piss myself off. I think if I die from anything it will be from embarrassment of what comes out of my mouth."

Mitchum's standard response to questions about the seamy side of his life draws a spur-of-the-moment remark like, "The rumors? They're all true. Booze. Broads. All true." Then: "Make some more up if you want to."

Mitchum cocks his head and squeezes one eye shut to avoid the curl of smoke from his cigarette, then continues, trying to soften what he has just said. "Hell, I've had hundreds of public relations flacks try to make something of me, to mold me, to design out of me the lump of clay I am not. They will do anything to get me in front of reporters. Why? Haven't they got enough on me already? Just let the writers regurgitate the words. It's all flack fat anyway. One reporter will gobble down everything I say, then poop it up, and the next one comes along and eats that up. Yeah, it would all be simpler if they all stayed at home and made it all up."

Ask how many lies have been told about him since he became an actor, Mitchum responds dryly, "Lost count long ago."

The actor rises, stiff-backed, his chest puffed out, and walks into the bar in the next room. The walk, like his sloe-eyed look—as one reporter wrote—"is part of his signature: pigeon-toed and charged with bored innocence, yet languid as a panther's glide." Another disgruntled reporter said, "Mitchum got his gait from trying to walk a straight line."

Mitchum plops the shot glass on the bar, and nods at the bartender. The white-hot liquid floods into the glass. A couple of heavyweights shoulder up to the actor, wanting to be next to his macho aura, next to Mitchum the two-fisted drinker, next to Mitchum the lady killer, next to Mitchum the brawler. One of them grabs the actor's hand in a wrestler's grip and asks him about his early professional boxing matches. Mitchum doesn't flinch, and the fight is on . . .

"I was boxing this guy in Wilmington," Mitchum says, tapping the glass on the bar. "This guy—he looked like the actor Van Johnson—was using me like a punching bag; I couldn't get away from his left hand. I finally got damned mad, and dropped into a low crouch." Mitchum demonstrates, his fists tight together: "I hit him on the inside of his leg." Mitchum lashes out viciously with his left fist. "It hurt him, he bent down, and I came up underneath—varoom!" He cuts loose with a looping uppercut that leaves its sting in the air. "That was it." Mitchum straightens his jacket and adds, "Long gone."

Mitchum's stint as a pro boxer is only part of his past. The six-foot-one, barrel-chested (forty-eight inches) "faggot's dream"—as he puts it—was also a rod-riding hobo: in the early 1930s his vagrancy landed him on a Georgia chain gang. "I was without a home and broke," he remembers, "a dangerous and suspicious character with no visible means of support."

After that he worked as a stevedore, a dishwasher, a jazz saxophonist, and even a songwriter. (He later wrote the songs for two albums, the 1957 Capitol release, "Calypso I Like So," and the 1958 "The Ballad of Thunder Road." He recorded the songs in his soft baritone, and both albums made the charts.) His career as an actor was slow coming.

Robert Charles Duran Mitchum began his act on August 6, 1917, in Bridgeport, Connecticut. His father, James, was a Scots-Irish mixture, his mother, Ann—as Mitchum once joked—was a full-blooded Blackfoot Indian. (She was Norwegian-born.) His father was killed in a railroad accident when he was eighteen months old, and when he was fourteen, he hit the road. "I left home because there was no room at the table," he says.

In 1940, three years before he got his start in the movies, he met and married an attractive, slim, dark-haired girl, Dorothy Spencer. Mitchum took Dorothy to Hollywood where they rented a $32-per-month flat. He got a job as a sheet metal worker, and Dorothy began to raise their family: Jim, born in 1941; followed by Christopher and Trina (Petrine). To provide for his growing family, Mitchum decided he could get work as a movie extra. "I was big and it looked like I could handle myself in a brawl," he drawls.

His first film was *Hoppy Serves a Writ,* opposite Hopalong Cassidy. In that one, and in the next six westerns he played in, he portrayed the villain, getting punched out in saloon fights. He didn't mind. "Hell, I was working in the movies, making one hundred bucks a week, plus all the manure I could take home."

In 1943 he took a step toward respectability with *The Human Comedy,* then two years later he was cast in *The Story of G.I Joe,* a role which won him his only nomination for an Academy Award. As is Mitchum's style, he didn't show up for the awards ceremony. "The Academy hasn't messed with me since." His smile shifts into a smirk.

The part of Lieutenant Walker in *The Story of G.I. Joe* was only one of many in which he played a military role. Cast comfortably in the military mold, Mitchum has been able to work his way through the ranks, wearing hats from all services: He was a Marine sergeant in *Heaven Knows Mr. Allison,* an Army finance officer in *The Big Steal;* a brigadier general in *The Longest Day;* a Navy captain in *The Winds of War* and *War and Remembrance.* He says his favorite role was as Admiral Halsey in *Midway.* "It was a one-day part and I got to play it in bed.

"Although I played all those military types, I feel I'm unclassifiable as far as casting goes. I am not really a leading man, not a comedian, and I'm not a heavy, although I think I can be most convincing as a heavy."

Mitchum went from being cast as the bad guy in westerns, to a war hero, to the cynical Philip Marlowe in *Farewell My Lovely,* to the tender-hearted sheep drover in *The Sundowners,* for which he was named best actor by the National Film Board of Review.

He feels he gave his most complex performance in *The Night of the Hunter,* in which he played a psychotic backwoods preacher with the word HATE tattooed on the knuckles of one hand and LOVE on the other, a sinister man who murders "sinful" women to get their money. In the film he also kills his wife, played by Shelley Winters.

"Best thing that ever happened to her," Mitchum says, warming the glass in one hand. "Shelley was all right in the movie, yet she was so insecure. Charles Laughton, the director, had to kick her ass to get her moving. I didn't think she fit the part of a wife in a small town, but I was the co-producer and when they said we could get her for a cheap twenty thousand, I agreed."

Mitchum crosses back to the living room, and steps up to the fireplace. The party crowd has now thinned to a dozen people.

"Charles Laughton watered the film down from what it was in the book," Mitchum continues. "The way it was written was terrifying. But Charles wanted to play the fairyland bit, and he photographed all the owls and bumblebees. He said he didn't want people taking their children off the street because the movie scared them so much. If I had been able to do it the way it was written, it would have been a sock-'em movie."

The Night of the Hunter was a macabre thriller, good enough, despite the actor's protestations, to propel Mitchum into almost any part he wanted, opposite any actress in Hollywood. "I never knew who I was going to be cast with," he says. "They just kept moving girls in front of me. I'd close my eyes and when I opened them, there'd be a new leading lady. Once I opened up and Marilyn Monroe was standing there."

The movie that matched Monroe and Mitchum was *River of No Return* released in 1954. When filming the love scene, Mitchum put his arms around Monroe's well-known body, then pulled her toward him while she looked up at him for a screen kiss, lips parted, mouth quivering. There was a breathless pause . . . then Mitchum backed away, shaking his head. "How in hell can I take aim when she's undulating like that!"

(Mitchum and Monroe became good friends. He had met her a dozen years earlier at a Lockheed company picnic. Mitchum's co-worker was a man named Jim Dougherty, who happened to be married to a pretty blonde named Norma Jean.)

Robert Mitchum's list of glamorous costars reads like a compendium of Hollywood beauty: Jane Russell, Rita Hayworth, Elizabeth Taylor, Angie Dickenson, Carrol Baker . . . His former costar, Deborah Kerr, observed, "He is a far more complex person than his lazy, relaxed manner would have you believe, a man who hides many lights under many bushels." Polly Bergen, who played Mitchum's wife in *The Winds of War,* said, "Bob Mitchum is the most caring, loving man I have ever met. He's always there for friends, but he doesn't play the phoney-baloney."

Not all of his costars agree with this appraisal. Katherine Hepburn found his bawdy jokes and macho mannerisms offensive. One day on the set of *Undercurrent* she stormed at him, "You know you can't act, and if you hadn't been good looking you wouldn't have gotten in pictures!"

Mitchum still roars with laughter over the quote. "Good looking?" he asks incredulously. "I came into the movies in the era of the ugly leading man that Bogart started. Before that, if you didn't look like Tyrone Power, you didn't work. After Bogie altered the image, I slipped in. The movie makeover people liked to ask, 'You ever think about getting your nose fixed?' I'd tell them, 'Sure, I had it fixed several times—by a straight left!'"

Mitchum is used to criticism. Early in his career he was awarded the least-cooperative "Sour Apple" trophy by the Hollywood Women's Press Club. He wired the women:

"Your gracious award becomes a treasured addition to a collection of inverse citations. These include prominent mention in several Ten Worst Dressed Americans lists and a society columnist's Ten Most Undesirable

Male Guests lists, which happily was published the date I was made welcome at the county jail."

Mitchum's "welcome" at the the county jail in 1948 was a shocker—he spent fifty days behind bars for possession of marijuana. Caught smoking a joint in a starlet's home (in what some say was a set-up), Mitchum was branded by a hostile press as a dope fiend. Preachers railed against him from pulpits, mothers hurried daughters past billboards of his films, yet he survived the adverse publicity. Instead of destroying his career as everyone expected, the marijuana charge just added fuel to it. Released from jail, he told a throng of reporters, "Jail is like Palm Springs without the riffraff. A great place to get into shape, only you meet a better class of people."

Mitchum has ignored most of the criticism heaped upon him. One story that appeared in the May 1955 issue of a Hollywood scandal magazine, *Confidential,* could not be ignored. The magazine printed an article reporting that Mitchum had attended a Hollywood party, and as he started on his second fifth of scotch—so the story went—he suddenly removed all his clothing, grabbed a bottle of ketchup, poured it over his body and shouted, "This is a masquerade party, isn't it? Well, I'm a hamburger!"

The slanderous story infuriated Mitchum and his wife. "We took them to court and proved it was a lie and a fabrication," Mitchum recalls. The million-dollar suit against the magazine was one of the many such suits that eventually buried the scandal sheet.

The Mitchums live as far away as possible from marauding reporters in a modest ranch-style home with a pool on three acres overlooking the Pacific in the chaparral hills of Montecito near Santa Barbara. What is overlooked is that Robert Mitchum is a family-oriented man. The Mitchums have five grandchildren. When not working on a picture, he says, "I answer the phone, open the mail, watch the evening news . . . "

When asked if he will ever spend his leisure time writing an autobiography, he shrugs, "What for? The Los Angeles police have it all on file."

He muses over this thought for a moment then adds, "Besides, everyone in Hollywood would have to leave."

Mitchum's disdain for writing his own book may come from several unauthorized autobiographies written about his life. "I hated them all," he says. "I remember one, the most widely circulated, and in the first paragraph, my wife's name is wrong, my birthplace is wrong, and my birthdate. Five mistakes in the first paragraph, and from there on it went downhill."

The question asks itself: Why hasn't he tried to correct these errors? "Why?" he shrugs. "I don't know any of my fans. Who cares?"

Mitchum picks up the last shot of tequila and smoothly, in a measured, prolonged sip, drains the glass. He smacks his lips and sighs, "Anyway, I've had enough trouble."

Mitchum's image, slightly tarnished, was polished to a new, deserving luster when he was honored with the Life Achievement Award of the American Theatre Arts. At the presentation dinner in Hollywood (which was attended by the who's who of the movie industry), film clips of his movies were shown, and letters of praise were read, including one from a man Mitchum always refers to as "Dutch": Ronald Reagan, then the President of the United States.

When the award was finally given, Mitchum nervously took over the microphone and spoke about his years in Hollywood, his 130 pictures, ending with the line, "I found a home and I never looked back . . . I've been on a long time." Then he looked at his watch and added with a smile, "Forty-one years, and three minutes."

Ruby Keeler

42nd Street Baby

"You're going to go out there a youngster. But you've got to come back a star!"

Come on and meet those dancing feet . . .
On the avenue I'm taking you to—
Forty-second Street!

UNTIL the 1933 triumph of Warner Brothers' *42nd Street,* the Hollywood movie musical was little more than a collection of production numbers with little, if any, story. Audiences were not going to put their hard-earned Depression quarters on the plate to watch a bunch of dancers parade around in a revue. (Rin Tin Tin had even got into the act, introducing—with an elaborate series of barks—the 1929 musical revue *Show of Shows.*)

The Warner studio issued a moratorium on musicals until someone could come up with a story line that was more than a series of song cues. A story was finally found—borrowed from the plodding 1929 musical *On With the Show*—and *42nd Street* was born. It created a sensation.

The musical boasted the talents of dance director Busby Berkeley; staid, solid Warner Baxter in the lead as the producer; Bebe Daniels portraying the prima donna; George Brent and Dick Powell as the love interests, and chorus girl Ginger Rogers.

It also introduced a new actress by the name of Ruby Keeler.

"'Ruby, how'd you like to go to Hollywood and work the picture houses for five days, maybe a week?' my agent asked. I had just signed with Mr. Ziegfeld to dance in *Whoopee* with Eddie Cantor, and rehearsals didn't start until September, so I thought—Hollywood. It sounded like fun. I was only seventeen, so I said, 'I'll have to ask Mama.'"

Ruby Keeler, now eighty-one, laughs at the memory, and plucks a cigarette from the package of Benson & Hedges and fires up the tip with a Bic lighter. She is seated at the dining room table of her Palm Springs home, her cane hooked over the back of a chair. She whisks the smoke away from her face with her fingertips and looks through the sliding glass doors at a fountain bubbling amid a profusion of tropical plants. The temperature at noon in the desert is 110 degrees; inside it is a comfortable 70.

In the adjoining sunken living room, in front of several white and mauve couches, is a large fireplace, above which hangs an oil portrait of Ruby, a vibrant, elegantly gowned actress. Today, as she recounts the past events of her life in the musicals, her features show the heavy wrinkles of her age, her hair coifed in tightly knit gray curls, her face a mask of chalky makeup. A year earlier she had a stroke which left her left leg and arm partially paralyzed. Still, she smokes incessantly, ignoring her doctor's warnings.

"Mama was with me day and night backstage, watching over me," Ruby continues. "Mama said she couldn't handle the train trip from New York, so I set it up with a girlfriend named Mary, who was five years older, to chaperone. On the trip I called her Aunt Mary. At that time, the trains took three days to cross the country and it was such a fancy way to travel. At different stops the dining car chef would buy fresh trout and cook it for dinner. Fanny Brice, who was going to Hollywood to do her first picture, *My Man,* for Warner Brothers, was on the train, so there was a big welcoming committee at the Los Angeles station. My agent from the William Morris office was there to meet me. Standing next to him was a gentleman I had watched in the movies, but had never seen perform on stage—Al Jolson.

"Jolson—who I had raved over in *The Jazz Singer,* the world's first 'talkie'—went up to Fanny Brice and gave her a big hug, to the delight of the publicity agents and cameramen. Then Fanny introduced me to Jolson by saying, 'This is Ruby Keeler.'

"Wow! Was I in awe.

"'I know *you*,' Jolson said, holding my hand. 'I saw you at Texas Guinan's place. You were that cute tap dancer.'

"Double wow! He knows me."

Ruby Keeler had started working at Texas Guinan's speakeasy in New York as a chorus girl when she was thirteen, celebrating her fourteenth, fifteenth, and sixteenth birthdays backstage. The dancers weren't allowed to sit with the patrons between shows or drink the bootleg booze. If anyone touched them, Texas Guinan, who was like a mother to her "girls," would usher him out the door. It was there that an agent spotted Ruby and told Mr. Ziegfeld, "There's a kid over there who's a great dancer." What Ruby didn't know was that Al Jolson had also seen her perform—and remembered.

At the train station Jolson didn't waste any time. He said to Ruby, "How'd ya like dinner tonight at the Beverly Wilshire?"

Ruby mumbled something about staying with "Aunt" Mary's relatives in Long Beach.

"I'll send my driver, Jimmy, to pick you up," Jolson replied.

"*And* my 'Aunt' Mary," Ruby stammered.

Jolson smiled that big wonderful Jolson smile, and Ruby could feel the entertainer's eyes watching her as she walked away.

Al Jolson and Ruby Keeler were married September 21, 1928. He was forty-two. Ruby was nineteen. Ruby went back to New York to dance in Ziegfeld's *Whoopee*. She was billed as Ruby Keeler Jolson, which made her husband furious. Not because Ziegfeld had used his name, but because Ruby was billed below Eddie Cantor. "How can you have a Jolson below a Cantor?" he told his wife. Jolson took her out of the show the next day. Ruby was learning to live with a legend. Undaunted, Ziegfeld cast Ruby in a new Gershwin stage musical, *Show Girl*, which also featured Jimmy Durante. She was a smash.

Later in Hollywood, Jolson got a call from Jack Warner.

Jack said, "I'm planning a new musical, *42nd Street* . . ."

"I don't think you can afford me," Jolson cracked.

"Jolie, the picture's not for you. I want Ruby to do it. It's a great tap dancing part for your leggy lady. She goes on, saves the show, you know, same old schmaltz, but a big production. We're budgeted for four-hundred grand."

Jolson hesitated. "Okay, but only if I'm her manager."

"Sure."

Jolson jolted Jack by saying, "I want $10,000 for her first picture."

"Ten thousand!" Jack screamed. "This is no gold mine."

"Yeah, but Ruby is." Hearing no response on the other end of the line, Jolson pressed on, "And one other thing—don't expect me to see her work. I don't want to watch her kissin' no other guys."

Ruby Keeler got her $10,000 and a 1930s partnership with Warner Brothers, Busby Berkeley, and a new performer uprooted from Pittsburgh, Dick Powell.

"I was like a scared rabbit in *42nd Street*," Ruby admits. "Dick Powell was too. I knew I wasn't an actress but figured all I had to do was say lines like 'What?' 'Who?' 'When?'"

She also had some real corny lines, such as the one she purred to George Brent: "Remind me to tell you I think you're swell." (Not all the dialogue was bad: Ginger Rogers as "Any-Time Annie" got the classic chorus girl line, "She only said 'no' once and then she didn't hear the question.") There was also the scene where Warner Baxter as the Broadway producer tried repeatedly to get Ruby to say the line, "Jim! It was great of you to come!" When she finally gets it "right," the line sounded no different from her first reading. No, Ruby Keeler wasn't a good actress, but she was a wonderful dancer. Warners would eventually cast her in nine more musicals, mostly with Dick Powell.

"I remember the chorus girls saying, 'Well, I would have got that part if I was married to Al Jolson,'" Ruby says, snuffing out her lipstick-stained cigarette. "Al never did get me parts. Sure, there were hundreds of other girls who could have done what I did. The only reason I was able to do it was because of Busby Berkeley, who was in charge of the dance production numbers. Buzz himself couldn't dance a step, but he had such a fertile imagination. He'd say, 'Try it, you'll do it great.' Then if it wasn't right, he'd tell me. I knew that he was trying to improve me, so I would try."

Several months after *42nd Street* was finished, Ruby did *Gold Diggers of 1933,* then *Footlight Parade,* which starred Jimmy Cagney. With Berkeley directing, she never knew whether she'd be sprouting out of a flower or dancing on a piano. One morning she walked onto the set of *Footlight Parade* and was shocked to see a huge pool of water with girls diving into it.

"I said, 'Buzz, I can swim a little, but I don't like to be under water. And I can't dive.'

"He said, 'You'll be able to do it. Get in the water with the kids, get used to it.'

"'Yeah, but after that, what do I do?' I asked.

"'For the first shot you'll go down to the other end of the pool and do a porpoise dive . . .'

"'A porpoise dive?' I knew I wasn't a fish.

"'Well, you dip your hands and you dive, then you swim underwater to this end of the pool with your eyes open because there's a window here with a camera. You have to time it so when you pop out of the water you're smiling.'

"Wow. Nothing to it. I said, 'All I can do is try.'"

Berkeley had a lot of champion Olympic swimmers diving off rocks. It looked dangerous to Ruby, with everyone swooping off different levels on top of one another. She was supposed to dive off a high rock, twenty feet high. Berkeley, realizing his actress's fears, had someone do the dive for her.

"I'd get under the water where the diver was supposed to land then pop up, smiling. I didn't like that," Ruby says, her face souring. "There were a lot of takes because I couldn't come out of the water on time. I had this long black wig they made me wear and it was always getting into my face. Buzz kept saying, 'I can't *see* you with all the hair in your face.' He finally got one take that looked pretty good.

"To set up the diving scene, Dick Powell crooned 'By a Waterfall' to me. Most moviegoers thought Dick and I were married, but the closest I got to him was looking in his face for seventeen choruses of 'I Only Have Eyes for You.'"

In *Footlight Parade* Ruby also had a big production number with Jimmy Cagney, "Shanghai Lil," which critics called one of the greatest musical numbers in film history. Cagney searches for his Lil in a sinister Oriental setting and Ruby finally pops up out of a barrel in Chinese makeup and says, "I miss you velly much a long time." Then Jimmy lifts her up on the bar and she dances. Ruby remembers it being "great fun to dance with Jimmy."

One day Jack Warner, cigar in hand, dropped by the set while Ruby was filming the "Shanghai Lil" number, mostly to joke around with Busby Berkeley. But he had something else in the back of his mind. He stuck around long enough to have his picture taken with Cagney, Berkeley, Dick Powell, and Ruby. Looking Ruby over carefully, Jack decided he would star her and Al Jolson in a musical together: *Go Into Your Dance* (1935).

"There were a lot of good musical numbers in it," Ruby remembers, "'About a Quarter to Nine,' and 'A Latin From Manhattan.' It wasn't any different working with my husband than it was with anyone else."

36

Jolson didn't feel the same way. The success of the movie called for a sequel, but Jolson feared comparison to his young wife and didn't want to end up as a husband-and-wife team. His ego wouldn't allow it. As Ruby says, "Al was called the greatest entertainer in the world. I know that was true because he told me so—many times."

Ruby's marriage to Jolson ended in divorce eleven years after their marriage. They had adopted one boy, Sonny, who has been with Ruby ever since, now happily tending the lush tropical garden that surrounds his mother's home.

Two years before the divorce, Ruby performed in her favorite musical, and the last one she did for Warner Brothers—*Ready, Willing and Able*. In it she danced on huge typewriter keys.

"It was difficult jumping from key to key doing wing-and-taps, and I'd get charley horses in my legs from dancing on those 'footstools.'" She lights another cigarette, inhaling deeply before continuing. "There was a solid black background. I had no idea that girls, on another set, lying on their backs and using their legs to tap out each letter, would be added to the final print."

She sighs. "I missed it when it was over. It was great fun." For a moment there is a sparkle in her eyes, a glimmer of a young Ruby waiting for her cue to go on. To dance.

After her marriage failed, Ruby faded from Hollywood's limelight. She remarried in 1941, and had several children by her second husband. Ruby's name was now Ruby Lowe. She didn't tell her children about her previous marriage or mention her work in Hollywood musicals. She was content being a wife and mother.

Then, in the mid-1950s the movie *The Jolson Story* was produced. Larry Parks was picked to play Jolson and Evelyn Keyes was cast as the entertainer's wife.

Ruby's mouth forms a firm line as she says, "That was ridiculous. I didn't want them to do the movie, and even asked Al not to let them film it because I was happily married. At the time his career was practically over, so he didn't listen. I told him I refused to let them use my name,

Ruby. He said okay, they'd use the name of another gem. I asked the William Morris office, my old agency, what I could do about stopping the production. They said, 'Ruby, you don't have a leg to stand on, they are going to do the movie without your permission. They can call the girl Pearl, or any other kind of gem name—and the audience will know it's you.'"

Ruby leans her forehead on the heel of her hand, absently twisting a gray curl. "I only saw the picture once—at least part of it. I walked out—but what I saw was awful. I wanted to hide. *That wasn't me.* That wasn't our marriage."

In 1979 Ruby's second husband died, and shortly thereafter she got a phone call from a producer in New York, Harry Rigby, who said he wanted to star her in a Broadway musical, a revival of *No, No Nanette*.

"I thought—this man is *nuts*. Me, go back to the Broadway stage at age sixty! I hadn't danced since the late thirties. I was thinking of saying no, then that evening I happened to watch an old TV movie and saw a young girl saying, 'All I want to do is go to Broadway and do a show!' I thought, You big dope, this gal is dying to go on stage, and you have the opportunity to do it.

"Well," Ruby continues, smoke curling in front of her face, "on opening night, before the curtain went up my children were all there— and they were embarrassed. 'What's Mom going to do?' they thought. 'All these people are here to see her—will she fall down, break a leg?' They hadn't seen my movies, nor did they know anything about my life as a dancer. I remember a kid once told my son, 'Johnny, I read where your mother was married to Al Jolson.' He replied, 'That's a dirty lie!'

"Anyway, I went on, didn't fall down, and my children were enthralled. *Nanette* played on Broadway for four years." Her brows furrow and a half-grin crinkles the corner of her mouth. "I guess you can say it was my swan song. But . . . I loved every minute of it."

Ruby Keeler's eyes have taken on a special luster as she remembers back to those wonderful days, dancing on stage, tap, tap, tapping in the movies, working with Busby Berkeley, listening to Dick Powell sing her love songs . . . and recalling that first big line that Warner Baxter said to her in *42nd Street:*

"Kid . . . you've got to come back a star!"

[Author's note: Ruby Keeler died six months after this interview, her last, was conducted.]

Barnaby
Conrad

James Stewart
"Ah . . . Waal . . . It's Jimmy Stewart"

"I never ran for government office because I . . . uh,
don't speak fast enough to be a politician."

I T IS early afternoon as I walk up to Jimmy Stewart's Tudor-style
home in Beverly Hills. A small van crammed with tourists on a "See
the Stars' Homes!" tour quickly comes to a stop in the street. They press
their noses against the van's windows and wait expectantly. I ring the
bell.

The door opens and Jimmy Stewart stands framed in the entryway,
looking as if he had just stepped out of a vintage Norman Rockwell
painting. His gangling six-foot–three-inch frame is attired in a blue
blazer, gray slacks, and a maroon tie; he blends perfectly with the Ivy
League feel of the brick house. Stewart shakes my hand; then seeing the
bus, he waves at the tourists.

"You . . . ah . . . waal . . . you'd better wave," he says in the world's
most imitated voice, a mixture of corn syrup, stammer, and pure fun. I
wave. Jimmy waves. The film fans grin wildly and wave back, their
shouts of "Hi Jimmy!" muffled by the sealed windows of the van.

"Well, now . . . come on . . . come on in," Jimmy Stewart says. He waves one last time then closes the door behind us. I wonder aloud whether over-enthusiastic fans ever get off the bus and knock on his door.

"Oh, sure," he says, leading me into the living room. His walk is the familiar Stewart gangling gait, like a circus clown on spindly stilts. "They . . . they want me to autograph something, or mostly just to say hello," he says.

"Doesn't that interfere with your privacy?" I ask. Then a different thought hits me: "Or do you feel you belong to the public?"

"Absolutely. I don't feel that my private life is my own. I must devote some of my life to my audience—my partners." He pauses. "Long ago someone told me that even though I might become a star in the movies, always remember this—never treat your audience as a customer, always treat them as partners. I've never forgotten that. It's . . . it's a tremendous piece of advice."

For five decades Jimmy Stewart's "partners" have applauded his down-to-earth qualities, both on and off the screen. Stewart is the ideal father who attended PTA meetings and marched in Boy Scout parades. He's the decent guy who has long been a staunch member of the Beverly Hills Presbyterian Church. He's the patriotic American who flew twenty combat missions in World War II. He's the nice guy who has never had a scandal attached to his name, and he's been married to the same woman for over forty years. Once described as "the most normal of all Hollywood stars," James Stewart is still the "aw, shucks" kid on the block, the "Mr. Nice Guy" in town, and "Everyman" to a world of fans.

Stewart's 1940 MGM Studio biography stated: "His type is as normally average as the hot dogs and pop at Coney Island." Moviedom's moguls capitalized on his ideal American appeal by casting him in parts that projected that image. His first big hit, *Mr. Smith Goes to Washington,* established him not only as "Mr. Average Nice Guy" but as an exceptionally talented actor.

In *Mr. Smith,* Stewart played Jefferson Smith, a decent, trusting person who by accident is appointed senator by the state's crooked party machine. The climax of the film is Smith's filibuster on the floor of the U.S. Senate to prevent his fellow senators from voting on his expulsion. The scene was a grueling one for Stewart.

"Grueling is as good a word as anything," Stewart remembers. "The hardest thing for me was trying to fake the hoarseness in my voice as the filibuster went on." As he recalls the story, Stewart begins to speak in a deep, gravely voice. "At the end of the day's shooting, the director, Frank Capra, came up to me and said, 'Jim, you don't sound as if you're losing your voice, you sound as if you're faking it.' Now that really worried me, so on the way home I stopped at an ear, nose and throat doctor, and went in and said, 'Is there any way you can give me a sore throat?'

"And he just looked at me kinda puzzled and said, 'I've heard you Hollywood people are crazy, but you take the cake. It's taken me thirty years to learn how to keep people from *getting* a sore throat and now you come in here and want me to *give* you one. Okay, I'll give you the worst sore throat you've ever had in your life!' So, I said, 'Well . . . fine.'"

The doctor agreed to go with Stewart to the movie set the next day, and every few hours would swab the actor's throat with a vile mercury solution that swelled and irritated the vocal chords. "I could hardly talk," Stewart remembers. "Hurt something terrible, but it worked!"

Stewart's acting tour de force in that film, aided by the medical profession, garnered a 1939 Academy Award nomination (the first of five such nominations). Stewart and Clark Gable (for *Gone With the Wind*) were rated as equal favorites to win, but Robert Donat took home the prize as the schoolmaster in *Goodbye, Mr. Chips*. A year later Stewart won the Oscar for his portrayal of a young newspaper reporter in *The Philadelphia Story*.

Whatever genre of motion picture Stewart has performed in, from westerns *(Winchester '73)* to mysteries *(Rear Window)*, from biographies *(The Spirit of St. Louis)* to love stories *(It's A Wonderful Life)*, he has never subordinated his own image to the character he portrayed.

When asked if he really plays himself on the screen, he replies, "I think I like Lawrence Olivier's answer. He said, 'I always play myself—with deference to the character.' I guess that's what I try to do too."

Jimmy Stewart stands quietly in his living room, surrounded by photographs and mementos of a life he has shared with millions of moviegoers. On the black surface of a grand piano are framed photographs of his wife, Gloria, and their four children; pictures of Stewart with Ronald Reagan, and a color shot of Gloria and Jimmy with Pope John Paul II. There is also a unique black-and-white photograph of Stewart standing by a painting of the six-foot rabbit, Harvey.

One of Stewart's outstanding portrayals was Elwood P. Dowd, the whimsical, pixilated companion of the invisible life-size rabbit, Harvey, from the movie *Harvey*, which was based on the English play by Mary Chase. "That's the only portrait of Harvey that's ever existed," Stewart says—"and it's gone. Somebody stole the original from a theater in London." His deep gray-blue eyes light up as he adds, "I guess I'm the only one today who knows what Harvey really looks like."

What *does* Harvey look like?

"Well . . . he's . . . he's upstairs," Stewart replies with a grin, and points at the ceiling. "I could get him for you. 'Course, he's taking a nap right now." He chuckles to himself. Perhaps I could chat with him after he wakes up.

"Ah . . . you see Harvey doesn't talk much until he's had his first cup of coffee."

Leaving Harvey at rest, Stewart leads me through a wide doorway into the adjoining library, saying, "You know, it's a funny thing, but I found this statue in a window of a store in China." From a coffee table he picks up a five-inch-tall filigree statuette of a rabbit done in delicate lace-like silver wire, a black bow tie around its neck. "I was told it's four hundred years old—but it looks just like Harvey."

Stewart puts down the statue and says, "I remember one time in New York I was walking along the street and a fellow came up to me—not very well dressed, and he hadn't shaved in a while—but he said in this quiet voice, 'Is Harvey with you?' And I . . . I started to make a joke of it, and then I realized it was a *serious* question. So I said, 'No, he didn't come this time. He's home with a cold.'" Stewart lowers his voice to a respectful whisper. "And the fellow said, 'Well, the next time you see him, give him my regards,' and he disappeared into the crowd."

Stewart is quiet for a moment as he recalls the simple, yet emotional encounter. Then, breaking the silence, he points to an oil painting on the wall and says, "Hank Fonda painted that. It's of my horse, Pie. He died two days after Hank finished painting it. I rode him for twenty years in my western movies."

A skilled horseman, Stewart made eighteen westerns, ranging from his first 1939 comedy role in *Destry Rides Again* with Marlene Dietrich, to a minor part opposite John Wayne in *The Shootist* (1976). As the "fastest slowpoke in the West," he also starred in such classics as *Broken Arrow, Cheyenne Autumn,* and *How the West Was Won.* Walter Brennan, who was often cast as his tobacco-chewing sidekick, once remarked, "Jimmy Stewart's not one of your rootin'-tootin', quick-draw cowpokes . . . Jimmy may look like he's dawdlin' along, but it ain't so. He's really one smart hombre. And straight as a hitching post!"

"In many ways, westerns are the most legitimate and colorfully dramatic tales of Americana," Stewart says, then adds, "I loved making them."

Stewart turns away from the painting of his horse and walks to a couch near a wall of bookshelves. "Well, I guess we can sit here. I call this 'my spot.'" Behind him on the bookshelf is a statue of an elephant. "Nice to have something conservative around," he says with a sly grin. Stewart is a staunch conservative Republican, and a close friend of Ronald Reagan. When asked why he never ran for government office, Stewart replies, "I . . . uh, can't talk fast enough to be a politician."

Stewart settles on the couch, hands folded in his lap. His fingers are long and delicate, better suited for portraying a pianist than a western sheriff drawing a six-gun for a shootout. I ask if his favorite movie was a western.

"No, a romantic comedy. *It's A Wonderful Life,* that was my favorite. I liked it because the story wasn't from a book, or a play, or a true happening, or a script developed by writers. It came from two sentences in letters that the director, Frank Capra, received from a friend. One of the letters had a P.S. that said, *Just remember, no man is born a failure.* Later, another letter carried this P.S.: *Nobody's poor who has friends.* The movie evolved from those phrases, and it fascinated me. The whole cast and crew had the feeling of being creative. It was very exciting for an actor."

Is there such a thing as a natural actor? I ask.

"I think so."

Are you?

"I don't . . . think so." Stewart responds slowly. "I mean acting doesn't come easy to me. I've always had great respect for it, because you can never sit back and say, well, I've got it made and I can play anything. You're always learning."

Do you ever get tired of playing Jimmy Stewart on the screen?

"I guess I can answer that the way Spencer Tracy did when asked the same question. He replied, 'What the hell am I supposed to do—play Bogart?'"

Who has been the greatest influence on your acting career?

"Josh Logan," Stewart says without hesitation. "Without him I wouldn't even be an actor. He was completely responsible for getting me into acting." Stewart leans forward, his elbows on his knees. "It was at Princeton, and I can remember exactly where it was on campus when Logan told me about the University Players. I can remember as if it happened just the other day . . . "

James Maitlant Stewart was born in the improbably named town of Indiana, Pennsylvania, on May 20, 1908. His father, Alexander Stewart, ran a hardware store and when customers didn't have enough money to pay their bills, he'd accept something in barter. One day a down-on-its-luck carnival troupe came in and paid with an accordion. "I just started fooling around with that accordion," Stewart remembers. "Every note doesn't have to be exact. You're able to fake a lot on an accordion."

Young Stewart also began to develop an interest in acting. When he was nine he put on a play called *Beat the Kaiser* in the basement of his home. "I played all the male parts," he says, "and my two sisters were Red Cross nurses. My dad saw us and it looked to me like he got sick from watching us act. Years later I realized he looked so red from trying hard not to laugh."

Stewart took his accordion along when he entered Princeton as an architecture major. Still interested in performing, he joined the school's prestigious acting organization, the Triangle Club, where he performed in several plays written and directed by a classmate, Josh Logan. Logan remembered that Stewart "genuinely liked being on stage, but it took him a long time to admit it. I finally asked him if he had ever thought about becoming an actor. 'Good God, no!' he shouted. 'I'm going to be an architect!' Well, he not only got a B. A. when he graduated, but an A.B.—Acting Bug."

"I hadn't seriously considered being an actor," Stewart recalls, "even up to that day I walked across campus enroute to get my degree in architecture. I figured I'd go home in the summer and work in my father's hardware store, then go back to school and get my master's degree. That's when I ran into Josh. I suppose it was the most important moment in my life."

Logan told Stewart about the University Players, a group of unknown young actors (which included Henry Fonda and Margaret Sullavan) who tried out Broadway-bound plays in a small theater in Falmouth, Massachusetts. Logan was directing the group and asked Stewart, "Why don't you come up to the theater for a few weeks this summer, bring your accordion and play in the tea room." Stewart figured it would be a good idea, and went.

"I lasted two nights in the tea room," Stewart says with a lanky shrug. "The people said my playing upset their appetites." Stewart hung around the theater sweeping floors, working on props and sets until

Logan finally gave him a bit part in a play. The one that he appeared in that summer was called *Goodbye Again,* which was moved to New York. The young student-actor-architect moved with it to Broadway. "I was on-stage for only a few minutes in the first act," Stewart remembers, "but I always came out for the curtain call. I could hear the audience whisper, 'Who's that?'"

Stewart decided to stay in New York, and after floundering around from job to job, landed a good part in the drama *Yellow Jack,* which put his name up in lights for the first time. Shortly after that success, he was offered a contract by MGM Studios. (His good friend and New York roommate, Henry Fonda, had beat him to Hollywood by seven months.)

MGM didn't know what to do with the lanky, 130-pound actor when he arrived at the studio in 1935. "He's a human giraffe!" one movie mogul cried. He was so skinny that the filmmakers decided to screen-test him as an emaciated Chinese man for *The Good Earth,* the movie based on Pearl S. Buck's novel.

Jimmy Stewart points to a picture on the wall taken from that test which shows him made up with a smooth-shaven head, a pigtail, slanted eyes, and dressed in a Chinese peasant's costume. "That's the first time I'd ever been made up," Stewart says. "I thought I looked great—even my own mother wouldn't recognize me. But as I was going to the studio commissary, everyone who passed said, 'Hi, Jim.'"

Stewart didn't get the part. "I was the tallest Chinaman you've ever seen," he says. "For the test, I had to walk in a trench beside the movie's star, Paul Muni, who tumbled into the ditch. They finally got a real Chinese who was five-foot-two."

The studio cast the young, gangly actor in comedies playing dull and dependable "other men" who always lost the girl. In one such film, *Wife vs. Secretary* (1936), he played opposite moviedom's blond bombshell, Jean Harlow.

"Harlow was a great kisser!" Stewart remembers, smacking his lips. "We had to do a romantic scene in the movie, and I'd never been kissed that way before in my whole life. I mean, boy, when Harlow kissed you, she *kissed* you." He grins and the boyish face from so many movies ago shines through. "Well . . . ah . . . you see we had to do the scene over and over, and by the time it was filmed, I was a very exhausted young actor."

Having yet to discover his average American image, the studio cast Stewart in a series of mediocre movies. In *After the Thin Man* (1936), he ended up the murderer, the only time in his career he played a villain. "Well, I just sort of tagged along in the movie," Stewart says. "The audience didn't find out I was the murderer until the last fifty feet of film."

He was even asked to sing in a film called *Born to Dance* (1936) with Eleanor Powell. One critic wrote that he sounded like "the hired man calling the cows in for supper." Stewart never sang in a movie again.

In *Ice Follies* (1939), Stewart was cast as an ice skater. "Lew Ayres and I were supposed to be figure skaters," he says, laughing at the image. "But when we showed up dressed in tights and skates, the director took one look at our legs and said, 'We'll have to change the story.' Instead they used us as a comedy horse. Lew and I flipped a coin to see which part of the horse each of us would be. I lost."

Then came the breakthrough movie—*Mr. Smith Goes to Washington*. Suddenly, the studio realized exactly what image Jimmy Stewart projected to audiences—a decent guy, an average fellow, the epitome of the honest, ideal American.

When he won the belated Academy Award for best actor for *The Philadelphia Story*, he called his father to say he'd won. Alexander Stewart told him, "That statue ought to look good in the store window." It stayed there until the elder Stewart died twenty years later.

Stewart's skyrocketing career was interrupted by the Second World War. He entered the Army as a private nine months before Pearl Harbor. Because he already had a pilot's license (he had taken flying lessons in Hollywood during the 1930s), he was sent to flight school and eventually became a squadron commander, flying twenty combat missions over Germany.

He is too modest to talk about his war exploits. "The war was just something everyone did," he says. He returned after five years a full colonel with a chestful of medals, including the Distinguished Flying Cross. He was promoted to brigadier general in the reserves in 1959, and he retired from the military in 1968.

He resumed his movie career in 1945, and continued to land parts opposite the most glamorous women in the history of cinema: Marlene Dietrich ("an absolutely stunning woman"), Lana Turner, Ginger Rogers, Paulette Goddard, and Olivia de Havilland.

I ask him which actress he found the most fascinating he worked with. "Grace Kelly," he says without hesitation. "She was an amazing actress. She had something that was absolutely her, something I had never seen before in an actress—or since. I worked with her only once, in *Rear Window*, which was directed by Alfred Hitchcock. It was a wonderful experience."

Stewart continues: "I guess the only real disappointment I've had in my career was because of Grace Kelly. MGM was doing a movie called *Designing Woman* and when I saw Grace Kelly was in it, I jumped at the chance to costar with her again. We were about to start filming when Grace went to L.B. Mayer and said, 'Mr. Mayer, I'm going to get married.' And L.B. replied (Stewart lowers his voice gruffly), 'Well, fine. We'll have a reception for you at the studio.' And Grace said, 'No, Mr. Mayer, you don't quite understand . . .' and she was off to Monaco!" He rubs his long fingers together. "They wanted to get someone else, but I told them I didn't want the part without Grace Kelly."

Although Stewart dated many of his costars, he remained the most eligible bachelor in Hollywood. That was until 1949 when, at age forty-one, he met and married a beautiful young woman named Gloria McLean and became stepfather to her two children, Ronald and Michael. Two years later, Gloria gave birth to twin girls: Judy and Kelly.

In 1969 the Stewarts suffered a crushing blow when Ronald was killed in Vietnam. "It was a terrible loss that we'll never forget," Jimmy says, the emotional loss still showing in his eyes. "But I can't look at it as a tragedy. The strength, the patriotic feeling, the bravery that he had—that takes the tragedy away."

Most people in "show biz" have been to the marital altar many times, yet the Stewarts' marriage has lasted over four decades. Director Frank Capra once asked Jimmy about the quality of his marriage. "He was silent a few moments," said the director, "then he scratched his ear and drawled, 'It's good . . . darn good . . . I guess it's that way because Gloria and I really like each other . . . and we're not afraid to show it.'"

Stewart rises from the couch and stretches his long legs. "Like to take a walk in the garden?" I follow him outside to an open adjoining lot he bought when the previous owner moved out. "I tore down the house, it was just plaster and chicken wire." He points to a large vegetable garden. "That's Gloria's garden. You know, you just forget how good tomatoes taste right out of your own garden." Stewart doesn't seem to be fazed by the fact that he grows his own produce in what may be the world's most expensive vegetable plot. Similar pieces of property in the Beverly Hills neighborhood sell for as much as a million dollars.

As we wander around the garden, the sunlight filtering through the trees, warm on our backs, Stewart tells me about his quartet of poems, *Jimmy Stewart and His Poems,* a thin volume that was published in 1989 and became a surprising bestseller.

"It was a happy accident," he says. "I recited a couple of the poems on Johnny Carson's show and a fan wrote me, suggesting I include them in a book. I thought about it, talked to Gloria, and well"—he grins— "another career was launched."

I ask what he might title a poem about himself. He smiles. "Why, *It's a Wonderful Life,* I suppose."

Walking back toward the house, I ask one last question: In one hundred years how would you like James Stewart to be remembered?

He pauses for a long time. "I . . . well . . . I've never been asked that before. I guess I really don't know." He thinks for a moment, then says, "People come up to me—it's happened so many times—and they say, 'I remember something you did in a movie . . .' and they can't remember what the picture was about, or where they saw it, or even its title. What they remember is something that happened, something that *moved* them.

Maybe it was just a look, or a word, an action, a *tiny piece of time* . . ."
He pauses. "I guess I just . . . I just want to know I've given people a
small piece of *time* they'll never forget."

A few minutes later Stewart opens the front door of his home for me.
As I step out, another van skids to a halt in front of the house, and the
fans wave wildly. I turn and look back at Stewart and he is smiling—and
waving.

Ronald Reagan
The Errol Flynn of the "B's"

> "Well, after I did that first screen kiss correctly, and the director yelled, 'Cut! Print!' well . . . I turned to the crew and said, 'I got news for ya, it was a helluva lot more fun at the high school picnic!'"

"**Y**ES," the press secretary told me on the telephone, "you can interview President Reagan—but you can't ask any questions."

What? Was the great communicator really the toothless grandfather figure with lapses of memory as portrayed in a cascade of White House memoirs? Were his well-known pauses and gestures in fact a sign that the gears in his brain had locked? After all, he would be celebrating his eighty-second birthday a day after the interview. *Why* was his staff being so protective?

No questions?

What the press secretary had tried to convey was that only *one* of us, Cass Warner Sperling, my collaborator on the book, *Hollywood Be Thy Name—The Warner Brothers Story,* or I, could ask the questions. (Cass is the granddaughter of Harry Warner, the president of the Warner Brothers studio during its forty-five years as a family-owned motion picture company.) Young "Dutch" Reagan had signed on as a contract player with Warners in 1937 and had made forty-three films for the studio, most of them as a leading man in "B" movies. Realizing that Reagan loved to spin tales about his Hollywood heyday, the interview had been set up and questions sent in in advance: no political queries, no fund-raising requests, just Reagan talking about his longtime reign as the Errol Flynn of the "B's."

•

Cass Warner and I arrive at the appointed time (we were scheduled for a half-hour interview) at Reagan's spacious penthouse offices overlooking the Avenue of the Stars in Los Angeles. The press secretary, an attractive young woman, ushers us past a secret service man with an earphone plugged into his ear (I was surprised that neither of us are searched) and into Reagan's office.

Ronald Reagan stands by his desk like a grinning wax museum figure, his face illuminated by the brilliant white light streaming in from windows that wrap halfway around the room. In a deft move, he grasps my hand and jerks me around for a grip-and-grin photograph: He holds his hand on my back so I don't move, I smile—and the flash goes off.

Standing side-by-side, I realize he is a bigger man than I had expected, tall and radiant, warm and relaxed. It is the oddest thing: It is not possible to be nervous in his presence. He gives the feeling that he's lucky to be with *you*. The first words out of his mouth are "Well, . . ." punctuated by the familiar nod of his head.

Reagan points out the view from his thirty-fourth-floor office: "Now, uh, well, that's Olympic Boulevard down there . . . bit smoggy today, the view gets obscured the farther you look south . . ." As he rambles on, I take note of the surroundings: a polished walnut desk with a neatly squared sheaf of papers in the center, a jar of red, white, and blue jelly beans, pictures of Nancy, one of the President and Mikhail Gorbachev shaking hands—then I return my attention to Reagan. He is bigger, broader than expected, a strapping six-footer in a blue-and-white plaid sport coat, complemented by a maroon tie. His hair, still thick, is streaked gun-metal gray. The only real concession to age is the hearing aids he wears in both ears.

He motions for us to sit, and the three of us settle into an L-shaped white sofa under the stark shafts of light. Reagan begins to tell stories about those first days at Warner Brothers, when, as a young radio announcer, he traveled to Hollywood on assignment to broadcast a Chicago Cubs baseball spring training session—and became a movie star.

REAGAN: "In Hollywood I happened to meet an agent, Max Arnow, who called a Warners casting director and said, 'I have another Robert Taylor sitting in my office.'

"The director answered 'God only made one Robert Taylor.' Well, he decided to take a look at me. After appraising me like a slab of beef, the director gave me a screen test reading a few lines from *The Philadelphia Story* with a Warner starlet, June Travis. I was told to stick around Hollywood until Jack Warner, the studio boss, had time to look at the screen test. Out of sheer ignorance, I did the right thing. I said, 'The Cubs are leaving for Chicago tomorrow and I'm going back with them to broadcast their games.' They hate to hear anyone say no, so after I'd been back in Chicago two days, I got a wire saying I had a seven-year contract with Warners at a salary of $250 a week, three times as much as I made as an announcer!

"The first thing they did was send me to the public relations department to give me a screen name. They sat around staring at me, thinking, What name does he *look* like? My mother had wanted to call me Donald but her sister had a son first and used that name so I was tagged with Ronald. I didn't care much for it. When I was a child I had a hairstyle that curled around my face with bangs so my father started calling me the Dutchman. I preferred that name and was called Dutch Reagan in high school.

"None of the publicity guys asked me what I thought I should be called so I said, 'At the radio station my name, Dutch, was well known as a sports announcer.'

"'Dutch Reagan? On a theater marquee? No way.'

"I sat for a minute then said, 'Well . . . Ronald?'

"'Ronald . . . Ronald Reagan. Hey, that's all right!'

"I was one of the few actors who got to use their real name."

Reagan grins, warming to his tale-telling, and crosses his legs. His green socks are ill-matched with the sport coat. The press secretary has pulled up a chair and is watching intently in silence.

"I had a Harold Teen haircut," Reagan continues, "a down-the-middle part, patterned after the hero of a popular 1930s comic strip. The makeup man took one look at me and said, 'Where in the hell did you get that haircut?' He insisted on combing it to the side. Then they put a bunch of makeup on my face. After a couple of tests, a cameraman told me, 'Look, you don't wear makeup well. You ever tried doing without it?' On the next test I did it barefaced and they said, 'That's it!' I was happy." He chuckles. "I didn't have to get up an hour earlier to be at the studio. I acted without makeup for the balance of my career."

Warner Brothers, like all the major studios of the 1930s, churned out two types of pictures: "A" movies which featured their major stars, and low-budget "B" films which featured newcomers. Reagan was assigned to the Warner Brothers "B" unit. His first film was *Love Is on the Air* (budgeted for $119,000), in which, ironically, he played a radio announcer.

REAGAN: "I had had no training as a screen actor and I was terribly nervous when I showed up. But once the director said 'Action!' I forgot all about the camera and crew and concentrated on saying the lines. To my surprise, when the director said 'Cut,' he was satisfied with the first take. Well . . . I got to thinking: Maybe I can make it here.

"My first on-camera kiss was with lovely little June Travis, who had helped me with my screen test. In the scene where the boy gets the girl"—Reagan pauses, his lopsided grin giving him an engaging, almost boyish appeal—"well, I *got* her, and *kissed* her. The director yelled, 'Cut!' and came over to me and said, 'You kissed!'"

Reagan nods his head. "I said, 'Well . . . the script said to kiss her, so I kissed her.'

"The director said, 'Yes, but you don't *kiss* her.'

"I scratched my head. 'What are you talking about?' What I didn't know was that the movies had designed a system of kissing. And that's why those love scenes in old movies are remembered. You embraced but you barely touched lips, so that you didn't push the actress's face out of shape. That made the most beautiful love scenes. Today, a kissing scene in a movie looks like they're trying to eat their way through each other.

"That's when I told the cast that kissin' was a helluva lot more fun at the high school picnic."

Ronald Reagan acted in thirteen "B" pictures in his first year-and-a-half at Warners. "B" pictures were usually only an hour long in comparison to an hour-and-a-half "A" movie. The "B's"—as Jack Warner said—were movies the studio didn't want good, they wanted by Thursday.

Brian Foy, the studio producer who was known as the "Keeper of the B's," bragged that he made one picture eleven times, using the same plot, just slightly changing the next version. He also cast the same actors over and over again in these movies, a technique that unsettled young Ronald Reagan, who grimaced when he learned he had been dubbed the "Errol Flynn of the B's."

Although he was happy being a movie star, he longed for a juicy role in a major production. In 1939 he did get one good part in *Dark Victory* starring Bette Davis and Humphrey Bogart. Unfortunately, that was followed by several more "B's" with titles like *Brother Rat and a Baby, An Angel from Texas,* and *Tugboat Annie Sails Again*. In each he costarred with a pretty young contract player named Jane Wyman, who would soon become the first Mrs. Ronald Reagan.

Three years after he'd started with Warner Brothers, he got his chance to play Notre Dame football hero George Gipper. Reagan worshipped football, a game he had played for eight years in high school and college. With this sports background he began to think that a movie on the life of Knute Rockne, the famous coach of Notre Dame, would make a great picture. Jimmy Cagney and Pat O'Brien would sit with

Reagan in the dining room at the Warners commissary and listen to him drone on about his great movie idea.

REAGAN: "One day I picked up *Daily Variety* and read where Warners had bought the life story of Rockne. I told Cagney and O'Brien, and they said, 'You talk too much. You've been all over the lot blabbing your story.'

"'I don't want to sell a story,' I said. 'All I want is to have the picture made and play the Gipper.'

"Cagney and O'Brien looked at each other, then me. 'Well, you better start talking to the producer because several actors have been tested for the part already.'"

Reagan shifts closer to the edge of the couch as if he is going to jump up and act out the next scene.

"Well . . . I stormed into the producer's office and said, 'Listen, this is the greatest football hero that ever lived; I want the role.' He looked me up and down, and then said I was too small for the part.

"'What you mean is I should weigh two hundred and twenty pounds.' I leaned over his desk. 'Would it interest you to know that I weigh five pounds *more* than the Gipper did when he played?' That wasn't getting me anyplace, then I remembered what a cameraman had told me: 'The only thing the fellows in the front office know is what they see on film.' I rushed home, grabbed my college football picture—there I was in full uniform—and hurried back to the studio. I shoved the picture in the face of the producer. 'Here, this is me playing football!'

"He looked at it and said, 'May I keep this for a while?'

"I wasn't home fifteen minutes when the phone rang telling me to be at the studio at eight in the morning for a screen test. Pat O'Brien volunteered to do the test with me and he ended up playing Rockne and I got the part of the Gipper."

Reagan wasn't in the picture a lot, but he did play one very emotional scene: The Gip is in a hospital bed, dying, and he says to Rockne, "Someday, when things are tough and the breaks are going against the boys, ask them to go in there and win one for the Gipper." As Reagan watched the preview, he heard the audience sniffling in their handker-chiefs. He thought, *Was this the acting breakthrough I had been wishing for?*

When Reagan arrived home the phone was ringing, telling him to report to the studio early the next morning. He had been cast as George Armstrong Custer in *Santa Fe Trail,* a historically inaccurate story of the attack on Harper's Ferry in 1860. Errol Flynn, playing Jeb Stuart, was the star but Reagan was the second lead in another "A" picture.

REAGAN: "When I was fitted with the military costumes for the movie, I noticed another rack of uniforms with the name, Dennis Morgan—Lt. Custer, tagged to each of them. A wardrobe man came in, took them off the rack, tossed them in the corner and replaced them with the gold-braided uniforms made for me. I thought, *That could happen to me someday.*"

Reagan leans forward and grins like he is about to tell a deep secret. "Errol Flynn—it was the funniest thing—he had a complex about his acting and was constantly worried that someone would steal a scene from him. Character actors didn't bother him, but the leading-man type—like myself—did.

"There was a scene in *Santa Fe Trail* where a newly commissioned group of officers from West Point gathered around a campfire while an Indian woman made designs in the sand telling us what our fortunes in war would be. I saw Flynn go up to our Hungarian director, Mike Curtiz, and heard him whisper, "Same uniform . . . move him." At the first rehearsal Flynn and I had stood side by side but now Curtiz called out in his heavy accent, 'I must line you up all again.'

"He took me and placed me behind two of the tallest fellows. I was standing on a downslope so the only part of me that showed over their shoulders was my forehead. As I stood there waiting for the shot to begin, I realized I was in loose gravel, so I started raking it into a pile with my boots. By the time Curtiz said, 'Action,' I had a gopher mountain built. I stepped on it—my head was now way above the other actors' shoulders—and said my one line."

Reagan chuckles as he relaxes back in the sofa. "Yes, you always had to watch out for Errol Flynn."

Although *Knute Rockne, All American* was the favorite movie he made for Warners, the one that he remembers as being the "classiest" was *King's Row,* a movie he considers to be his "finest acting effort." It starred Ann Sheridan and Robert Cummings, and Reagan played a young man who loses both legs in a train accident. One reviewer reported: "The acting was so splendid that the movie confounded the cynics who had assumed that Ann Sheridan and Ronald Reagan were too lightweight for their roles."

"Yes," Reagan says with a wistful look in his eyes, "*King's Row* was the best picture I was ever in."

World War II erupted, but before Reagan joined the military, he did one patriotic film, *Desperate Journey,* which also starred Errol Flynn. This time Reagan stole the show with his portrayal as the wise-cracking co-pilot of a B-17 crew shot down over Germany. It would be 1947 before Reagan made another movie.

Concerned with what his future might be at Warners and discontented with the movie roles Jack Warner had given him before the war, Reagan hoped to return as a leading man in "A" pictures. It was a forlorn hope.

REAGAN: "I always said this about Hollywood: If you were a sailor in a picture that made money, then buy yourself seasick pills because you won't see land again for years." He laughs, his cheeks turning red. "I had been pretty successful with the drawing-room comedies, the Cary Grant type of roles, but I wanted to do a western. I started bellyaching all over the studio. Finally I went to see Jack Warner, and said, 'If you ever let me do a western, you'll make me a lawyer from the east.' Instead of getting angry, the next thing I knew I was cast in *Stallion Road.*"

Reagan was excited because he was going to costar with Humphrey Bogart in a Technicolor film about horses. It wasn't exactly a western, as he played a veterinary surgeon, but it did have horses! A week before shooting began, Bogart dropped out and was replaced by Zachary Scott.

Jack Warner decided to shoot the picture in black-and-white. Reagan was back doing second-rate movies.

Reagan shakes his head as he remembers that movie—and the following one: "I was next cast in *That Hagen Girl* in which Shirley Temple starred in her first grown-up role. Sure enough, Jack Warner cast me as a lawyer. I played Shirley's lover but audiences weren't ready for the Lolita aspect of the story. My favorite role of that period was . . ."

He pauses and gestures with his hands, deep in thought, but is unable to recall the name of the movie. We wait. The press secretary quickly goes into action: She takes a movie encyclopedia from the bookshelf and begins thumbing through it.

Before she can dig out the movie title, Reagan recovers: "Well, let's see . . . yes, it was *The Voice of the Turtle* based on John Van Druten's play. I portrayed a lonely soldier who woos Eleanor Parker." Back in control now (the secretary closes the book, but still holds it at the ready on her lap), Reagan laughs: "In that movie I was caught with my pants down.

"You see, each year the studio gave a party and editors of the different films would save some of the funniest out-takes. Well, in this one scene with Eleanor Parker, I was supposed to change out of my uniform into civilian clothes, so . . . well, I was directed to step behind a chair to make the change—but on each take the pants zipper stuck. I tugged at it behind the chair and finally walked before the camera, saying, 'The damn zipper's stuck.' That happened several times until the crew was in hysterics."

As Reagan winds down his movie career—the last film he made for Warners was the 1952 bomb *She's Working Her Way Through College*, in which his costar, Virginia Mayo, played a stripper turned college student—I glance at my watch. An hour has passed and I can hear murmurs outside the door, the subdued voices of his next appointment. One last question is asked: "What would you like people to remember about you as an actor?"

"I like being remembered as the Gipper," he says without pausing. "I have a Notre Dame sweater and, believe it or not, it was Gip's. After I became president, I was invited to address the school's graduating class and was presented with Gip's letter sweater. It now hangs at the Presidential Library next to my Eureka College football letter sweater."

The room is quiet. Reagan looks at us, then slowly rises. "Well . . ." He gestures with the palms of his hands as the secretary gets up and stands by the door. In parting, I ask him to autograph a copy of his autobiography, *An American Life,* that I had brought along. As he sits back down, pen in hand, I add, "Would you mind inscribing it: 'Write one for the Gipper?'"

He grins, that lopsided grin again, and says, "I've never written that before," and adds his "Ronald Reagan" squiggle as he finishes the inscription.

Outside the office, book tucked under my arm, several secretaries crowd around, saying, "You know, we've never heard him having so much fun. It's wonderful for him to laugh."

As I walk toward the door, I notice an open jar of stars-and-stripes jelly beans on the secretary's desk. I pop one in my mouth.

Definitely an "A" flavor.

Barnaby Conrad

Jane Russell
Gentlemen Prefer Brunettes

"In the movies—me! Today? There's too much sex and nudity. I would never have done a nude scene. I even refused to wear a bikini that Howard Hughes had designed for me in *The French Line*. Too embarrassing."

"**I** WANTED a nice classy portrait on the jacket of the book," Jane Russell says holding up a copy of her autobiography, *My Paths & My Detours*. "My publishers convinced me this *thing* in the haystack from my first movie, *The Outlaw,* was *the* Jane Russell people wanted to read about."

She drops the book on the coffee table in front of her and sighs, "I'm sick of the picture."

On the full-color, wrap-around cover, Jane Russell is shown reclining seductively on a stack of hay with her skirt lifted high on her thighs. Her peasant blouse is pulled tightly across her ample bosom, and her mouth is pouting sensually. "I always looked like I was wrapping gum around my teeth," she adds, glancing one last time at the book.

Today, relaxing in the living room of her home, feet raised high on her favorite recliner, a cup of coffee warming her hands, Jane Russell is far from the image portrayed in the scandalous 1940 photograph. Having passed the seventy-year mark (Russell was born in 1921), she has opted to wear a baggy lavender and gray jogging outfit and gray leather tennis shoes for today's interview. She looks comfortable, not seductive.

"I *like* to be comfortable," she says, her voice raspy, its timbre not yet attuned to the early hour. (It is eleven in the morning and she admits to not being a day person.) "It wasn't that way when I first started making movies. I was utterly miserable in the clothes Howard Hughes had the studio designers dream up for me to wear. The costumes were boned, stiff, strapless—and uncomfortable. I wouldn't put them on until the scene was ready to be shot."

Russell sips from the coffee, then sets the cup on the coffee table, which is cluttered with magazines, opened letters, a notepad and several pens. She has reluctantly applied the day's makeup, deep red lipstick and fake eyelashes, and brushed her hair, which is streaked with thick waves of gray.

"Hey, nobody's perfect," she says, plucking at the jogging outfit's jacket. "I'm certainly not. I've never worn a dress under size fourteen, and the least I've ever weighed is one hundred and thirty-five pounds. I'm a full-figured—'generous' may be a better word—short-waisted woman."

She smiles at that and settles deeper in the lounge chair, her face illuminated by a wall of sliding glass windows that lead to a redwood deck and view of oak trees. One thing unusual: there are no photographs of the actress on the walls, no museum of Jane Russell memorabilia; no glossies from *The Outlaw*, color enlargements from *Gentlemen Prefer Blondes*, or the 1955 hit *Gentlemen Marry Brunettes*. Not even a theater poster from the Broadway musical *Company*.

Where were the photographs of Russell with Clark Gable in *Tall Men*, Robert Mitchum in *Macao*, Bob Hope in *Paleface*? What about the studio publicity shots of her in the startling sequined one-piece swimsuit she wore in *The French Line*, or the bikini that Howard

Hughes designed for her in the same movie? Where's all the movie-star stuff?

"Oh, I've done that," she says in a rumbling growl. "I've been in the movies, and it was all illusion. That sexy broad on the screen really wasn't me."

Fifty years ago, with the release of *The Outlaw,* Jane Russell became the most famous sex symbol in America. Howard Hughes's five-year publicity campaign that preceded the movie's release had made her face and figure synonymous with lust and desire—everything that good boys of the 1940s were not supposed to think about.

"They were selling Jane Russell," she says. "It was like slapping a label on a can of tomatoes."

To the moviegoer of the fifties and sixties, Jane Russell was a long-legged, lushly proportioned, sensual fantasy. In real life she was a teenage tomboy who loved to climb trees and slide down haystacks with her four brothers. She was the girl next door, the girl who married her high school sweetheart, football legend Robert Waterfield, and lived happily for twenty-three years. She was also the mother of three adopted children: Tracy, Thomas, and Buck.

Early in her marriage, her deep love for children led her to found the national adoption organization, WAIF. Working with Eleanor Roosevelt, Russell was able to get the Orphan Adoption Amendment of the Special Migration Act of 1953 passed. Because of it, children who had been accepted for adoption could enter the United States without being restricted by immigration quotas. In 1977, WAIF started concentrating its efforts on locating parents for orphan children in the U.S. In little over thirty years WAIF placed 36,000 children.

Jane Russell's primary goals were never her movie career or stardom. She preferred her close relationships with her friends, her family, and most of all her personal faith in the Lord. "The Lord is a living doll!" she once said, and was widely quoted by the press.

Russell's personal references to "the Lord" are a bit disconcerting—she autographs copies of her autobiography, "Jane, who loves the Lord.

God bless!"—and far from her celluloid image as a bad girl. Did she have difficulty selling her autobiography to a publisher because of her beliefs?

"Sure!" she answers emphatically. "I had to go from publisher to publisher until I found someone who would leave in most of the stuff about the Lord. The book is my life story, and there was no way I was going to let anyone take the Lord out of my life. The Lord is the main cornerstone of my existence."

And what are Russell's religious beliefs?

"I hate the word religious," she says, as if the word leaves a bad aftertaste. "To me it means there is too much formality in the church. I like the story where Jesus is walking along and he sees a little black boy sitting on the steps of a massive, silver-domed cathedral, and Jesus says, 'What's the matter, sonny?' And the kid is crying as he answers, 'They won't let me in there.' Jesus nods. 'Well, don't feel bad. They won't let me in either.'"

She laughs, then adds, "You see, my belief is based on the Bible. That sounds like fundamentalism, but it isn't. I don't preach to anyone. If someone asks me, I just say, 'Know the Lord!' That's what I tried to say in the book."

She glances again at the cover of the book, perhaps wondering if that girl on the cover really is her, then shakes her head. "The book came out pretty good, except for the two hundred pages they cut. After the editor at Franklin Watts read it, he told me, 'Okay, you've covered the Lord, and your family, three marriages, and your career, but we just can't go into all these friends!'"

She sighs. "They took a lot of fun out of the book, and I think it became too serious. My marriage with Robert Waterfield lasted twenty-three years. Twenty of those years were happy, but the book was edited to focus on the three bad years. Those were the years that were dramatic. After all, how often can you describe a perfectly nice, happy day? I was lucky to get in one page about the normal days of the marriage."

Although Russell claims to prefer a quiet home life to the glamour of a movie star, she admits she is far from domestic.

"I can't cook!" she says. "My first husband and I had a perfect arrangement—he did the cooking, I did the dishes. I sat on the sink while he prepared the food and we'd talk over what he did with the Rams football team that day—he was the teams' quarterback and eventually the coach—and I'd tell him what I did at the studio."

She stuffs her hands in the jacket of her warm-up outfit and slouches deeper into the sofa. "The first thing I ask a man is if he can cook. It works, too—I married three great cooks." (Russell was divorced from Waterfield in 1965. Two years later she married actor Roger Barrett, who died tragically only three months after the wedding ceremony. In 1974 she wed John Peoples, a real-estate investor. It is Peoples who collects memorabilia of his wife. In a guest house near a pool he has hung an array of publicity photographs and posters of Russell's movies.)

"Several years ago," Russell continues, "an editor wanted to do a photo layout with me in the kitchen. My husband, John, told them that would be the biggest joke in the world. 'Get her out of the kitchen,' he yelled. Oh, I made Eggs Benedict once, but I got the hollandaise out of a can." She throws up her arms. "I—don't—want—to—cook!"

Would you rather be in motion pictures again?

"In the movies—me! Today?" she says, wide-eyed, as if a toad had just asked for a kiss. "There's too much sex and nudity. I would never have done a nude scene. I even refused to wear the bikini that Howard Hughes had designed for me in *The French Line*. Too embarrassing."

Did you like yourself in your first movie, *The Outlaw?*

A long pause, then a deep breath. "I thought I was . . . slow. Wooden." She squirms. "Look, I'm not the hysterical type. I don't move quickly. I take things easy." She throws her arms up and admits the truth. "Okay! I'm *lazy*. I had a marvelous Russian drama teacher who once told me, 'You know, Jen, you could be a very good acktress, but you haff no energy.' And it's true: on the screen I seem to be moving in slow motion.

"In *The Outlaw*, I was terrible. But," she adds defensively, "I have to blame a lot of it on the direction. We had to do each scene over and over again, maybe ninety takes, until it got to the point where I wasn't allowed to raise my eyebrow or lift my shoulder. There wasn't anything natural about my movements. That wouldn't have happened if Howard Hawks had stayed on as director. It could have been a wonderful movie."

That must have been very disappointing.

Another pause. "Yes . . . very. Howard Hughes was the producer. It was his picture, and he kept interfering with Hawks's directing, telling him what to do, what he liked, what he didn't, so that finally Hawks blew up and said, 'Okay, Howard, direct it yourself!' and left.

"Unfortunately, Howard decided to do exactly that—direct *The Outlaw*."

How did a nineteen-year-old girl with no acting experience get selected for a starring role in a Howard Hughes movie? Like many movieland stories it began with a photograph. A Hollywood photographer happened to see Russell, thought she had a "look," and took some pictures. Through an agent, the photographs ended up on Hughes's desk, and he just happened to be searching for a new face to star in *The Outlaw*. Jane Russell, along with four other girls, was selected as a finalist.

"For that screen test, we were all dressed alike in peasant blouses," Russell remembers. "We were all brunettes, and we were all nervous. Then it was my turn. Honestly, the camera didn't bother me—the lights were so intense that the people standing around faded away—and I knew my lines, so I said them. That's all."

Howard Hughes was not present at the screen tests, and it was two days before Russell received a call that the film's director, Howard Hawks, wanted to see her, along with a new actor, Jack Beutel, who had auditioned for the male lead.

"At first Hawks didn't say a word," Russell says. "He just sat behind a desk looking at Jack and me. Then in his slow, quiet way, he said, 'Well, you two kids have the parts. Mr. Hughes has looked at all the tests over and over and you're our decision.'"

Once Hughes's new sex symbol was signed to a contract, he went about making her the publicity event of the decade.

"Oh, yeah," Russell grimaces. "I was supposed to be a poor Cinderella who had been lifted out of poverty to become a movie star and was helping to support her mother and four brothers. Little did the public know that I could barely make my car payments and eat on my starlet's salary of fifty dollars a week, let alone support anyone."

During the publicity campaign, the shooting of *The Outlaw* continued under Hughes's plodding direction. There was one major problem—his star's bosom. A custom-made brassiere would have to be constructed to best show off Russell's bustline under the peasant blouse. Hughes decided it wouldn't be any harder to design a brassiere than it would be an airplane. He would design it himself.

"A Mr. Playtex he wasn't," Jane says dourly. Then she stops, reluctant to go on. "I'm really sick of that bra story."

Please go on.

"How about an alternate story?" She rolls her eyes, a gesture right out of her sassy character, Dorothy, in *Gentlemen Prefer Blondes*. "In 1937, when I started wearing bras, department stores only sold items with nasty little cutting straps with no give to them at all. Even as 36B, which I am, I endured deep red lines on the shoulders and back. When a suffering friend directed me to a shop on Hollywood Boulevard where they sold comfortable custom-made brassieres, I happily paid more."

She grimaces as she continues with the *Outlaw* story. "Howard tried to design a seamless bra, which was way ahead of its time, but when I tried it on I found it uncomfortable and ridiculous. I wasn't going to do a hundred and three takes with it on, so I put on my own bra, covered the seams with tissues, pulled the straps over to one side, and went out to do the scene. Everyone behind the camera stared. Howard looked closely, then finally nodded okay. I never wore his bra—and he never knew it."

Howard Hughes's relationship with his new sex symbol was platonic. Whether he wanted it that way is doubtful, but his shy overtures were met with stoic resistance from his newly married star.

"I was later told that Howard confided to a writer that I terrified him," Russell says. "Howard said he wasn't going to fool around with a married woman, especially one married to a football star. That's a laugh. That poor, darling man afraid of *me!*" The eyes roll one more time. "Sorry, folks, another legend shot down."

She quickly adds, "On thing . . . Howard wasn't a weirdo. He was kind and considerate, with a child-like sense of humor."

It is obvious that Russell had a lot of affection for Hughes. Was she disturbed by his macabre death?

"I think there was . . ." Her voice lowers to a whisper. "I think there was some dirty pool going on. Those men that were keeping him didn't help him when he needed it. And all the people who *did* care were not allowed to see him. How could that beautiful, strong-willed man let it happen? Unless"—she pauses—"they got him on drugs."

Jane Russell is quiet. A faint mist glistens her eyes. Howard Hughes was too much a part of her career to be forgotten. Hughes kept her under contract for most of that career, loaning her out to other studios for special movies. One of those was the very successful *Gentlemen Prefer Blondes,* co-starring Marilyn Monroe.

"The press tried their best to work up a feud between us," Russell remembers. "But they were sniffing up the wrong tree. When the movie was released, the reviews were great. They headlined us 'The Haystack Brunette versus the Blowtorch Blonde,' then agreed that we worked well together.

"Marilyn was sweet, shy, and very serious, and would stay for hours after the day's shooting, working with her drama coach. On the set, I was usually made up and ready to go before she was. I'd drop by her dressing room and say, 'Come on, Blondy, let's go,' and she'd say, 'Oh, okay,' in her whispery voice, and we'd walk on the set together."

And how was it acting with Robert Mitchum?

"I did two movies with Mitch," she answers, "*Macao* and *His Kind of Woman,* and he was great to work with. He never made a mistake, was totally professional. I know he was the image of Peck's Bad Boy, but that's just the devilment in him. When visitors would come on the set, he would do something to shock them. He said they had come to look at the clowns and he wasn't going to let them leave disappointed."

And what about Clark Gable, Russell's co-star in *The Tall Men*?

"He was a doll to work with, and a terrible tease. I loved him." She reflects for a moment. "You know, I never had any clashes with my leading men. I guess I really love working with people. That's why I enjoyed the Broadway musical *Company*."

Company, which opened in 1970 with Russell in the lead role (replacing Elaine Stritch), helped her achieve the critical success that had eluded her in the movies. One reviewer wrote, "This debut may well mark the beginning of a whole new career as an actress whose celebrated attributes up to this time have been only her cleavage."

"I have never been so happy with myself as when I was doing *Company*," Russell says. "Thirty years after my debut as an actress in *The Outlaw*, I had opened on Broadway and received rave reviews. As my Mom would say, 'Praise the Lord!'"

Performing in *Company* also led to a contract with Playtex. "While I was doing *Company*, the Playtex people asked me to be the spokesperson for their company's brassieres. They agreed I would be a natural. I knew Betty Grable had done a girdle commercial for them, and it was to be done in very good taste. Besides, the product was something I've always believed in—bras!"

She picks up her autobiography, takes one more look at Jane Russell sprawled on the haystack, the actress with the sensuous pout that looked like she was wrapping gum around her teeth, then slaps the book back on the table, and adds: "You know, I was always a tomboy. I've mentioned climbing trees with my brothers, sliding down haystacks, riding horses . . . but at six years of age, I also found the Lord. If I could sum up my life, I guess I'd say that I was just—one of the boys who found the Lord."

Barnaby
Conrad

Rod Steiger
Running Hot and Cold

"Someone once asked me what's the best side of my face. I said, 'My ass.' I can't be concerned about that stuff. I haven't got the kind of face to worry about."

IT WAS one of those days," Rod Steiger says, his eyes half-closed, dreamily, thinking back, "a day when I woke up feeling good, a day when I woke up feeling *balanced*. The Chinese have a great respect for the word, balanced; when you're in balance your philosophy is stronger. I'm antiwar, and *that's* the day they sent me *Patton*. I told them I'm against war and I'm not going to glorify a general."

He sighs. "If I had been half as good as George C. Scott, I would have walked into the part of *The Godfather*. That's right, Steiger, not Brando. Hell, I did the Kleenex-in-the-mouth stuff on television in 1947 playing an old man." He purses his lips. "I would have been very hot if I had played in *The Godfather*—and the heat would have still been with me. I would have gotten better offers."

His brows furrow, and the eyes ignite. "Look, the child in me wants it good all the time. I don't want to hear all this up-and-down crud. *I want it good every day.*"

Rod Steiger's intense, penetrating style of acting has won him accolades from the public and critics alike, but he has not always found it easy to adjust to what he calls "the hot times and the cold times" of his acting profession.

In his long acting career, Rod Steiger has gone through periods of "hot times" with such movies as *On the Waterfront* and *The Pawnbroker,* both of which earned him Academy Award nominations. His sizzling performance as the redneck police chief in the 1967 movie *In the Heat of the Night* won him the Oscar for Best Actor. But there have also been "cold times" when he appeared in such clinkers as *Duck, You Sucker,* and the 1988 television movie *The Desperadoes.* "Don't remind anyone about that one," he whispers.

Steiger is on constant lookout for a warm front to show up on the horizon, and thought he had it in 1989 with director Norman Jewison's *The January Man.*

"I was really excited about that one," Steiger says. "That was the movie I had been waiting for. Hell, even *it* turned out to be a goddamn stinker."

Steiger crosses his legs and leans back. He is sitting in a circular, carpeted conversation pit in a rented house in Malibu while his nearby home is being refurbished. He wears a short-sleeved plaid shirt, which billows over his khaki pants, and loafers worn without socks. He is an intense, earthy man, devoid of the usual Hollywood plastic and gloss. His hair is almost white, his features rough and rubbery, the creases pressed deep by time and his explosive changes of expression.

On a shelf is the Oscar he won for in *In the Heat of the Night*—covered with a glass bell jar. "The salt air pits the gold," he says.

Steiger admits he has made his share of errors picking movie roles. "Yeah, I've done some terrible pictures," he says. "Those are psychological mistakes you make trying to show people that you're still alive. I've been told by my agent that people don't know whether I'm dead or alive so I'd better go to work. I have accepted bad scripts whether I liked them or not."

His shoulders sag. "I'm walking down the street and somebody says, 'Hey, you're on television tonight!' and I ask, *'The Pawnbroker?'* They say, 'Naw, *Vengeance.*' And you die, because it's like cancer. I thought I had that cut out. I thought I was rid of it and they're bringing it back tonight."

Because of the hot and cold times of his acting career, Steiger has suffered several bouts of deep depression. The worst came, not from a bad movie, but from the time he underwent heart bypass surgery in 1976. "I was so depressed after my operation, I plotted suicide," he says. "You just kind of say, I'm nothing, nothing interests me, and nothing ever will and I will never do nothing again."

The actor planned how he was going to carry out the suicide: he would row out to deep water in a boat, lean over the side, put a gun in his mouth and blow his brains out. When asked why he didn't simply shoot himself in a bedroom, he answers, "I didn't want anybody to be upset with the mess."

It was this thought that made Steiger realize he wasn't serious about suicide.

"When you're really suicidal," he shrugs, "you don't worry about anybody cleaning up the mess."

Steiger is contemplating writing his autobiography, and even knows how it would begin—at the point when he underwent heart surgery. "I don't want to write a Hollywood actor's book," he says. "I want to write my book. It would be a collage and would start with a man being taken out of a hospital bed; he's rolling down a corridor counting the fluorescent lights, going into the surgical room to have open heart surgery—and his life begins to flash by in his head." Steiger uses his hands expressively, pointing out each sequence of the story. "His childhood would be here, his first sexual encounter here, his old age here . . . Look, we're writing about a human being who's going in for an operation that scares him to death." Steiger begins enunciating each word as he has done in so many movie roles: "And—facing—death—he—thinks—about—his—life. How—he—first began . . ."

Rod Steiger began his life in Newark, New Jersey. Not once in his school years did he consider becoming an actor.

"I became an actor because I was chasing girls," he says with a thin smile. "I had completed a five-year hitch in the Navy and was working in a civil service job when I noticed that all the girls in the place were disappearing on Thursday nights. Someone said they were meeting with the civil service theater group, so I joined, hoping to get lucky with the girls. I did a couple bit parts and the director told me I ought to take acting seriously. I said, 'You're kidding.'"

Steiger decided to give it a try and went on to study with the New York Theater Wing, then the Dramatic Workshop, and finally Elia Kazan's Actors' Studio. It was Kazan who offered him the role of Charlie playing opposite Marlon Brando in *On the Waterfront*.

Steiger says, to this day, that his most memorable scene is the one in the back seat of a taxi when Brando says, "I coulda been a contender." For his portrayal Steiger got his first Academy Award nomination—and his first taste of Hollywood studio mentality.

"I always thought one of the biggest mistakes this town ever made—and I think it shows a certain stupidity—was not casting Brando and me in another picture right after *Waterfront*." He opens his arms wide, his eyes incredulous. "It was ridiculous. If I was a producer at that time, I would have said to get these two guys together again. Here you have two young bulls locking horns, let's see them fight again."

Because they were never cast together again, Steiger admits he has not seen Brando. "It's not that we have been feuding," Steiger says, "but I remember being very hurt because he wouldn't read lines for my closeups. I always acted offscreen for his closeups. Hell, that's what a professional actor does. I had to play the scene with an assistant director saying the lines."

He leans forward as he continues talking about Brando. "Look,

Brando's one of the greatest screen personalities in the last fifty years." Steiger holds his hand up like he's halting a truck. "I'm not saying he's the greatest actor. In my opinion he doesn't have a long range. Give him a part that's close to him like Stanley Kowalski in *A Streetcar Named Desire* and he's great."

Steiger shakes his head disgustedly as he recalls another disappointment in his acting life. "Why didn't they do a sequel with Sidney Poitier and me after the success of *In the Heat of the Night*? And another thing, when they cast Carroll O'Connor to play my part on the television version of *In the Heat of the Night*—Howard Rollins took Sidney Poitier's role—I called Sidney and I asked, 'Did they talk to you about this TV thing?' He said, 'No, they never called me,' and he asked if they had talked to me." Steiger gives a tiny shrug. "I don't think either one of us would have agreed to do the roles, but we sure would have liked to have been cuddled."

Although *In the Heat of the Night* holds a special place in Steiger's list of highs and lows, he had expected to win the Oscar a year earlier.

"I thought I was going to win for *The Pawnbroker,*" he says. "When they announced Lee Marvin in *Cat Ballou,* I almost fell over. I was angry, and I have to say this—in all honesty—I was furious."

Yet, even after winning the Oscar, the good offers and better scripts were slow to come. Using his versatility as an actor, he accepted roles playing such notable characters as Mussolini, W.C. Fields, and Napoleon. Although he says that he searches for the essence of the person he portrays, his research into Napoleon's character went deeper than before: He studied Napoleon's autopsy.

"I was able to get hold of a French copy of it," he says. "The autopsy was done on a billiard table! This may seem like a crude way to put it, but I got to know what this guy was like from the *inside*. Napoleon's body was dying and his mind was still alive. From that report I got the concept of how to play him. I even added a little scene in front of a fireplace where he says, 'Oh, God, my mind is alive and my body is dying.'"

Steiger feels he can play any role, that he's not trapped into being just a personality or a "single image" actor. "I hear actors say, 'That's not good for my image,' and I feel like tapping them on the shoulder and saying, 'I'm sorry *you* only have one image. You're supposed to be able to create all sorts of images. You're supposed to be all sorts of people.'

"Young actors learn to talk and listen—and that's all they do. Acting is supposed to be an exploration of life. You're supposed to have the guts to take a chance. You don't play it safe, you try to explore."

No one can doubt that Rod Steiger has the range to play any part. And play it well. On the movie screen one can look into his eyes and see the inner thoughts of the character. It's like opening the pages of a novel and reading how the character feels, thinks . . .

"To get that inner feeling I try to personally identify with the situation as if it's happening to me," Steiger says. "I become the character. The problems are personally mine—Rod Steiger's. In the movie *January Man,* I played the mayor, whose daughter is threatened by a killer. I don't want my daughter to be killed, and to feel that emotion I think of my daughter, Anna. I did scenes thinking, 'This guy slapped my daughter,' and the director says, 'Jesus, you can get mad!'

"There are times when you become so intense that it can be frightening," Steiger continues. "In the movie *No Way to Treat a Lady,* the phone rings—I've got one line in the script where I'm talking to a detective who's trying to catch me—and I say the line, 'How do you like that? Wasn't that nice, you got another dead woman on your hands . . .'" Steiger lowers his voice to a whisper. "And I went on for thirty more seconds improvising until at the end I was screaming with hostility. We cut and there was dead silence on the set. Nobody knew what I went through, but they knew something had happened. The director asked if I wanted to shoot the scene again and I said I wouldn't shoot that again if my life depended on it. I realized it showed something sick in me, this maniac inside of me came out. And—it—scared—me—to—death."

He swallows, remembering. "Directors who know me just say, 'Keep it going.' When I did live television in the 1950s they never turned the camera off until I had finished. They'd say, 'He's going to do something

82

at the end of this scene . . .'" He grins thinly, thinking perhaps that he's revealing too much of himself, then shrugs. "Sometimes you make an idiot out of yourself."

Rod Steiger is a movie actor, the camera and crew his only live audience, yet he approaches each scene as if saying lines for a thousand theatergoers.

"An actor has to be a little bit of a ham, and if there's nobody on stage to watch him except a cat, then he wants that cat to purr by the time he's finished. On a movie set there's maybe fifty people standing around behind the camera. I don't look at the director, I watch the electrician to see if he lowers his newspaper while I do the scene. If the director says that was wonderful the way you moved your hand, then you shut your mouth and take the credit. 'Really? Glad you liked it.'" *Sotto voce,* Steiger adds, "'When'd I move the hand? I don't remember doing that.'"

Thinking it over, he adds, slowly, "Sometimes after you've done a scene, you end up with a memory to survive with when you get older. It's what I call the narcotics of acting. These great moments when a performer is feeling the deepest emotion he can feel and the audience feels it at the same time. You both stumble on it unplanned, unrehearsed, unexpected. That is what I call *moments*. And if you get that ten times in twenty years, then you must be one of the greatest actors on earth. I've had it a couple times—and I'm hooked. *And you want to get it again.* It's like getting a fix. Like being on a high."

In 1986 Steiger had one of the high points, not of his career, but of his personal life, when he married for the fourth time. (His first wife was British-born actress Claire Bloom, whom he married in 1959 and by whom he has a daughter, Anna Justine. He later married actress Sally Gracie and horse-handicapper Sherry Nelson.)

"Several years ago I went to a dinner with my daughter and across from us was this very distinguished looking seventy-year-old gentleman with this very young girl. I was attracted to her immediately and wondered what this beautiful girl was doing with this older guy." He laughs.

"I should talk—I was with my daughter. And then the man introduced himself—and his daughter, Paula. Our eyes met for the first time, and we were in trouble. You couldn't walk between us, you'd hit the beam going from eye to eye, and it'd knock you on your face."

Steiger begins speaking in a rush, the words tumbling over one another. "So, when she went to the ladies room, I got up and cut her off and said, 'I haven't got time to fool around, I just gotta tell you I'm going to leave town the day after tomorrow, and do you want to have dinner tomorrow, yes or no?'" He takes a deep breath. "Paula's thirty-four years younger than I am—but that's all right."

Steiger smiles, a satisfied look on his face. Life hasn't been bad to the actor. The heady moments in the spotlight have brightened the clouded corners of his life. Besides, who knows what the next day may bring? Who knows what movie offer might come along. Perhaps something George C. Scott turned down on a day when he woke up feeling *balanced*.

Who knows? It might be the right movie.

The hot one.

Jane Seymour
Miracle Woman

"I'm fortunate. I'm working with an instrument, the camera, that loves me. I'm definitely not the prettiest or most beautiful person in the world."

"QUEEN of the miniseries?" asks Jane Seymour, and she smiles, tiny, perfect rows of white. "Well, it certainly was nice to be queen of something!"

Jane Seymour's bewitchingly wicked portrayals of a string of naughty ladies on television screens during the 1980s and 1990s cinched her claim to the mythical royal crown. One critic dubbed her the "epitome of evil" for her portrayal of the sinister Kate in *East of Eden*. Another reviewer said: "She was terrifying. I don't care how pleasant she is in real life; she must have found something awful inside of her to play from."

Seymour agrees. "I definitely think there are 3 million of them! I have a lot of people inside of me, and I am so blessed to be in a profession where people pay me to discover these people."

Her most recent character discovery has been her portrayal of Dr. Michaela Quinn, a liberated Boston-bred physician who revolts against her stifling background by heading west to Colorado Springs, where her enlightened ideas and compassionate ways win over the townspeople—as well as millions of today's television viewers. The show, "Dr. Quinn, Medicine Woman," which Seymour considered a risky bet at first, turned out to be an immediate hit, the highest-rated program in its Saturday-night time slot in more than ten years.

"I thought it would be a wonderful two-hour movie—something I was used to doing—and that would be it. I'd never see Dr. Quinn again." She pauses, remembering her original impression of the character. "To play the part was a gut reaction. I don't consider myself an intellectual, but I knew instinctively who Michaela Quinn was. I identified with her. I could be her.

"The show is not a soap opera melodrama," she continues. "Nor is it the standard cowboys and Indians shoot-'em-up, or the mushy stuff found in 'Little House on the Prairie.' The story of Doctor Quinn has love, action, heart, and humor." Seymour adds, "I also liked 'Dr. Quinn' because the show deals with today's issues, yet the stories take place in the 1860s. We have filmed shows that focus on Indian problems, the homeless, life-threatening diseases, alcohol abuse. I have been deeply touched by the series."

Seymour leans forward on the patio table and folds her hands. Her arms are delicate. Her eyes are remarkable; one is shaded brown, the other green, an uncanny and disturbing feature. The actress's voice, with its subtle English overtones, has the clipped, grassy quality of a woman constantly on edge, a woman trying to exert complete control over her existence, a woman waiting, impatiently, for the next event in her life. It's hard to imagine her totally relaxed.

"One of the reasons I decided to do the series is to get more clout," she says. "I still intend to make terrific movies. But frankly, when I look at the movies coming out today, I don't see many female parts that I would consider. I will not do what actresses like Sharon Stone have been doing recently. I'm not making a moral issue of it, it's simply about privacy. Certain parts of my body have been seen by a great number of people"—she did a *Playboy* pictorial several years ago and posed for what the magazine termed "bewitchingly wicked" portraits—"and other parts will always have a smaller audience." She smiles wickedly.

Now in her early forties, Jane Seymour has retired her old image as a high-toned Harlequin heroine for her new persona as a frontierswoman. What is it about this intense English actress that makes her come alive in front of the television and movie cameras?

"I'm fortunate," she says. "I'm working with an instrument that loves me. I'm definitely not the prettiest or most beautiful person in the world." (One smitten cinematographer disagreed, "Wow . . . if Bo Derek's a ten this lady's a ten-and-a-half.")

"There are many women who are more spectacular looking—but the camera does find *things*," Seymour continues. "If I do nothing, if I don't move my face, if I just think about something, the camera picks it up and broadcasts it loud and clear. The camera sucks these things out of me."

The question seems to ask itself: "Do you like your *acting* on the screen?"

"Oh, no! I'm never pleased with anything I've done," she says. "I've always criticized my acting. I take the whole thing apart."

Seymour says she is very selective in accepting the parts she plays, and agrees that she has made few mistakes. "Well," she smiles, "there was one I turned down four times, *War and Remembrance*.

"That was in 1988 and at the time I was not prepared to go away from my husband and newborn baby for filming nine months in Eastern Europe," she says. "Then I read the script—and cried through the whole night. I couldn't put it down. I was obsessed with it."

The grueling nine months on location in Eastern Europe filming *War and Remembrance* were more than Seymour had counted on.

"It was exhausting, horrendous, and depressing, immersing yourself in those terrible times." Seymour sighs, and smoothes her blue-and-white polka-dot skirt across her knees—the *same* skirt she wore while filming the concentration camp scenes. (Like all of the clothes Seymour wears in her films, the skirt is part of her prized costume collection.)

Hanging over the skirt is a baggy white knit sweater that drapes from her shoulders. Scuffed ballet slippers complete her interview "costume."

Seymour is sitting at a redwood picnic table on the patio of her Santa Barbara, California home (which she sold in 1993). A line of shadow from the overhead latticework falls over her carefully made-up face and angles across her hair which is parted in the middle and hangs straight to her shoulders. Her eyes glow intensely as she recounts the arduous months of filming at Auschwitz, the infamous Nazi extermination camp.

"I am very proud to have been in *War and Remembrance,*" she says, quietly. "It was more than an acting piece; it was a crusade."

In ABC's lavish adaptation of Herman Wouk's novel—the title of the book refers to the fact that the beginning of the end of war lies in remembrance—Seymour portrayed Natalie Jastrow (originally played by Ali MacGraw in *Winds of War*), an American of Jewish heritage who finds herself a victim of Hitler's persecution. In the episode of *War and Remembrance* aired in November 1988, Natalie and her uncle, played by Sir John Gielgud, found themselves interned in a ghetto, an interim stop enroute to Auschwitz.

"Even now I can't watch the scenes we shot in Auschwitz without trembling," Seymour says, wiping a bead of perspiration from her brow. "During the filming we would lose all comprehension of being human beings. There was a presence in that place of something horrendous having happened." She shakes her head sadly. "I swear you could even smell the dead flesh.

"Many of the extras in the film were real survivors of the death camp," Seymour continues. "Some of them still had the identifying tattoos. Most of them were Eastern-bloc Jews who had never been in a movie, and we made everything so real they believed they were back in camp. In one scene a woman next to me, who had been interned in Auschwitz at age twenty-six and survived, had tears rolling down her face. As we were filming, she looked around and whispered, 'This is *real*.'"

Seymour says she has memories of stumbling half-naked through scenes in sub-zero weather. In one particular instance, she was hosed down with water and left covering her breasts in a room filled with naked, shaven-headed extras. "You're so demeaned, you feel like cattle," she recalls.

She shivers slightly as she remembers the reality of the scene. "The women's heads were really shaved. In the shower scenes everyone was stark naked—even Sir John Gielgud. Then the gas chamber . . . I know that Sir John and I, and the people we worked with on the film, put everything into it. I . . . I am very proud of the work I did."

She pauses, then adds, "My mother spent four years in a Japanese concentration camp in Java in World War II."

Seymour's parents—her father a London surgeon, and her mother a Dutch concentration camp survivor—named their daughter Joyce Penelope Wilhelmina Frankenberg. Joyce, early in her career, changed her name to that of Henry VIII's third wife; now even her family calls her Jane. Her parents noted that as a child she was different from her two sisters, Sally and Anne. "If Jane wanted to do something, she didn't ask, she didn't cry, she just did it," the actress's mother recalled in an interview.

What Jane wanted more than anything else was to be a ballet dancer, even though she knew her body was built "totally wrong" for ballet. She is only five-foot four-inches, but consoles herself: "I have a long neck and carry myself well from dancing, so I think I look taller.

"I was told early on that I was not built for classical ballet," she says, "but I was such a high-achiever, I made my body do more than it could tolerate." At age seventeen, while dancing professionally in Covent Garden with the Kirov Ballet Company, she suffered a knee injury that ended the dancing career.

"As a dancer, I was never technically brilliant," Seymour says. "All the reviewers said everything happens 'up top.' They would say, 'A fine dancer, *and* a very sensitive *actress*.'" Seymour rises from the table and stretches gracefully. You can see that dance is in her body—you see it in the way she sits, the way she moves her neck, the way she walks through her films. "Since I couldn't be a dancer," she adds, "I decided to become an actress."

Seymour began to perfect her acting craft. In Britain she took to playing every kind of role she could: a striptease artist in *Not Now, Darling;* Winston Churchill's first love in the film *Young Winston,* and even the classic roles of Ophelia in *Hamlet* and Nora in Ibsen's *A Doll's House.* Her big movie break was as Solitaire, the sex symbol, in the James Bond movie, *Live and Let Die.*

Then it was off to America where she languished for a while in such potboilers as *Dallas Cowboy Cheerleaders*—until her luminous star quality began to glisten. The actress was nominated for her first Emmy in the 1976 television special *Captains and the Kings,* but she feels she gave a better performance in the 1981 version of John Steinbeck's *East of Eden,* portraying the venomous brothel owner, Kate.

"Kate haunted me totally," Seymour says. "I really began to feel I was her, and it took me weeks to get out of her. I had her anger inside of me. It's not a part I'd like to play every day of the year, as it could destroy my life."

Then came her role as Hemingway's racy Lady Brett Ashley in *The Sun Also Rises;* identical twins (one psychotic) in *Dark Mirror;* the part of the flame-haired Victorian artist in CBS's *Jack the Ripper,* and her portrayal of opera star Maria Callas in ABC's *Onassis: The Richest Man in the World.* For that role she won the Emmy for outstanding supporting actress in a miniseries special.

"I was quite astounded to hear about the nomination for Callas," not-so-plain Jane Seymour says in her lilting English accent. "I thought I might be nominated for my part as the Duchess of Windsor in the series *The Woman He Loved.*" Then came the acclaimed miniseries *War and Remembrance.*

Seymour is a great defender of the miniseries. "I believe they are the art form of our time," she says. "They offer the chance to present to the vast public book adaptations that they would never otherwise know. I also think they encourage people to read and reread the classics."

Seymour scorns reminders that her huge successes on the tube out-strip the successes of her big-screen movies. "Most feature films today are for seventeen year olds, prize fighters, and vigilantes," she says in swift response. "The best roles are in television."

When asked how many miniseries she has been in she is genuinely stumped for an answer, but thinks it's "around seventeen, most of which I have really enjoyed."

Seymour is also pleased with another product of her talents—her book, *A Guide to Romantic Living*—"written more or less to have something to do" when she was three months pregnant with her second child, Sean.

"I'm not a writer," she says. "I've never taken a writing lesson. I don't know anything about writing books. But I do know how to express myself, and that's what I did. I wrote it with anything I could find, which in my house is often a child's crayon."

She excuses herself, rises from the patio table, walks into the house and returns quickly with a copy of *A Guide to Romantic Living*. Her photograph is on the cover, a picture of a fantasy princess in a silk gown trimmed in pearls, a lake and a white swan in the background. The book is lavishly illustrated with color photographs of Seymour in elegant costumes, many of which she wore in her movie and television roles.

"I wrote the book for the person who wants to live romantically," she says. "Take someone you love and go to the beach, watch the waves roll in . . . don't wait for a holiday. Surprise the other person. Do it! Whatever your romantic dream, do it. You see all those cards showing a couple walking the beach at sunset? Well, don't buy the cards—walk the beach first, then send the card.

"Even the disasters that have happened to me when I tried something new have been some of the most romantic moments of my life. On my wedding day I decided to do my hair up in tiny braids and entwine them with real flowers. On my wedding night I found myself and my husband desperately trying to undo the braids. There was no way"— she gig-gles—"we could dive under the covers with dead flowers in my hair."

For many years Seymour lived life out of her own romantic book: handsome husband, David Flynn, a financial consultant for top showbiz personalities; two lovely children, Katie and Sean; owner of a sumptuous fifteenth-century manor house, St. Catherine's Court, in the English countryside; and a skyrocketing career as an actress . . . Then it all went sour. The rigors of a career and family did not mix. Jane and David were divorced in 1992. Jane Seymour's romantic fantasy had ended. But only temporarily. Romance returned to Seymour's life in 1993 when she married James Keach, the director of "Dr. Quinn, Medicine Woman." Keach also directed his wife in an ABC movie, *Through Hazel Eyes,* based upon the true story of a small-town Mississippi newspaper publisher who fought for civil rights and won a Pulitzer prize in 1964.

Even with her marital problems, Seymour likes to say, "My life is way beyond any dream I ever had."

If one movie role captured her romantic and nostalgic image best, it is her favorite as the turn-of-the-century beauty in *Somewhere in Time.* "That film was very much me," Seymour says. "I'm not sure I believe in a past life, but I feel comfortable in that era. There's something very strange . . ."

She opens her book to an oval photograph taken for the movie showing her in a Victorian dress. Next to it is another oval photograph, a turn-of-the-century portrait of Seymour's Dutch grandmother in a similar pose. "My mother found this picture of my grandmother in the bottom of an old drawer years after I'd finished the movie. See the amazing similarity."

She closes the book, then continues. "*Somewhere in Time* had an enormous effect on people and was one of the reasons I wrote my guide to romantic living. I guess I feel more at home in the Victorian era than I do today."

And does Jane Seymour want to continue acting when she's eighty?

"Oh, yes! I must have something to do with films, television, or theater. I love it. I thrive on it. Like Helen Hayes and Ruth Gordon, I think people who work until they are older are much happier."

Step aside for the "dowager" queen of the miniseries.

Barnaby
Conrad

Bo Derek

Home on the Range

"When I fuss or talk back too much, John says he's going down to the local high school and find another one."

"ISN'T he magnificent!" Bo Derek says leaning farther over the rough rail fence of the corral. "He's a Spanish horse, an Andalusian breed. Look how fast he's going, he's flying!" She claps her hands ecstatically. "See the fire in him? *I love him.*" She continues to watch as the spirited animal kicks up plumes of sand, and tosses its head arrogantly in response to the trainer's silent demands.

I turn from the horse's performance and focus my gaze on Bo Derek. Her cheeks are a bright pink from the crisp Santa Ynez Valley air, and she has on a head scarf, a felt hat, a heavy sweater, jeans and boots, and a bulky nylon jacket. She looks like a bundled-up *Peanuts* character ready for an outing on an icy pond.

Except, she *is* beautiful. "I don't consider myself a '10' in any way," she had told me earlier. "But everyone involved in the movie tried to create an *illusion* of absolute beauty. Nobody can be a perfect '10' because everybody's standards are different."

It was the 1979 movie *10* that turned Bo Derek into an American icon of beauty. After the film's phenomenal success, she entered an orbit of her own where she could grasp anything she wanted. She was immediately offered a $5-million, two-picture deal. She turned it down. "John and I felt we wanted control of ourselves," she says. "We decided to make *Tarzan, the Ape Man*—together."

In that jungle movie Bo appeared as a nude, sexually assertive woman opposite a Tarzan whom critics referred to as "nothing more than a spear carrier." Because of her nude scenes, Bo was dubbed, "Little Bo Peek," and "Peek-a-Bo."

John Derek's critics accused him of exploiting his wife's spectacular figure. He answered matter-of-factly, "God assembled her brilliantly. It's what she feels and thinks and does *without* her clothes that makes her exciting and attractive."

In person, without makeup, bundled up against the cold, and animated from observing her favorite horse, Bo Derek, now in her mid-30s, is considerably more beautiful, softer looking than she was in *10* or *Tarzan*, or *Bolero*. She has the aura of an angel, wide-eyed, excited, and a bit astonished with her first trip to earth.

"He's dragging his hind legs," John Derek says, edging next to his wife at the corral's rail. He stares intently at the horse being maneuvered in tight circles. "Look at him kicking up the sand. He's being lazy." John Derek, an expert horseman, brushes a strand of gray-white hair from his deeply-tanned face. Thirty-two years older than his wife, with his graying beard and penetrating stare, he is beginning to look more and more like a Hemingway character. Formidable, with a sharp cutting edge to his personality which he tries—usually unsuccessfully—to blunt, Derek is constantly besieged by a hostile press. After a heart attack in 1989, which left him somewhat dazed by his own mortality, he prefers to relax on the Dereks' ranch near Santa Barbara, occasionally writing, producing, directing, photographing, and editing soft-core sex comedies starring Bo, such as the ill-fated 1990 release *Ghosts Can't Do It*.

In *Ghosts*, Bo once again titillated the cast, which included Anthony

Quinn and Don Murray, with her Venus-like body. Donald Trump, who had a cameo as Mr. Spectacular, said he did the film because he and the Dereks are friends and "it was fun looking at Bo." After the movie died at the box-office, the Dereks slipped deeper into their home-on-the-range lifestyle.

Shoulder to shoulder, John and Bo watch their prized stallion for a few more minutes then Bo shivers and says, "It's really getting cold. I'm a beach girl and not used to this." The temperature, unseasonably brisk for the Santa Ynez Valley, is forty-seven degrees.

As she and John walk toward their Spanish-styled ranch house, John bends down and picks a purple wild flower, then pulls Bo toward him and puts the flower in the headband of her hat. It is a warm, affectionate moment, one of the many they say they have shared in their marriage. "I'll go in and put a couple logs on the fireplace," he says, turning toward the house.

Continuing with Bo on a tour of the stables, I ask how she and John have managed a May-December marriage which a critical press predicted would fail.

"We have the same likes and dislikes," she says with a grin that heightens her high cheekbones. "Neither of us smoke or drink; I've never been one for parties, neither has John. He has lived his life much longer than I have, and very fully, and I enjoy learning from him."

She pauses, then answers my unasked question. "The age difference starts getting smaller. People ask me what I will do when I get old, and I tell them I don't care what I look like. As for John . . ." she smiles a wicked little smile, "I'll just take away his glasses."

In front of the stables she pauses for a moment to hug the neck of a white mare, purring into the animal's ear, "Ummm . . . pretty baby."

She continues: "John and I have a good support system. He worries about me, I help him." She laughs. "When I fuss or talk back too much, he says he's going down to the local high school and find another. It's all a joke and we both understand it."

John Derek's first marriage was to French actress Patti Behrs, by whom he had two children. His second walk to the altar was with actress Ursula Andress, who was followed by Linda Evans, both of whom bear a striking physical similarity to Bo. All three have high cheekbones, delicate features, square shoulders, a tiny waist, and—as one *Playboy* writer noted—"identical rib cages and generous bosoms." Because of these similarities, John Derek has been accused of being a self-styled Pygmalion, molding his wives to his own emotional, physical, and intellectual specifications.

"Oh, the press has been insisting since we were married that John is my Svengali," Bo says. "I wish he were. I wish he did make all the choices for me. It would be a lot easier. But he won't. He says: 'It's up to you; it's your decision.'"

To thumb their nose at the incessant Svengali criticism, the Dereks named their production company Svengali, Inc., and listed Bo Derek as president. Then they asked artist Frank Frazetta to design special stationery. Lying on her stomach across the top of the full-color letterhead is a flesh-toned drawing of a nude Bo Derek manipulating puppet strings from which dangles the limp form of John Derek.

Bo stops at a corral next to the stables and calls to a white, and very pregnant, Andalusian mare. "She's Spanish, with such a pretty head," Bo says, kissing the horse's neck. "Look at her big black eyes." The mare turns away satisfied with the attention. Bo whistles softly after her. "She's going to have a baby in April. She gets bigger every day."

A wild assortment of dogs, eight of them, bark and tumble playfully with each other on the grassy hillside near the Dereks' house, "Why did you decide to move to the Santa Ynez Valley?" I ask as we walk toward the side door.

"Funny, but we used to visit the area in our van and we'd stop at a Solvang parking lot to sleep. We both thought we'd live in this valley someday." She looks at the two-story white house with its typically red-tiled Spanish roof. "When we first drove up here, we knew without looking at each other that this was the place."

She turns and gazes across the rolling hills of their forty-eight-acre ranch, past the stables and the corral, where the trainer still guides the stallion through its paces, to the gray layers of clouds beyond. "I could just stay here all the time," she says wistfully. "I love it here."

We step inside the house which isn't any warmer than the outside. John walks in with a firewood log the size of a tree trunk and dumps it in the fireplace on top of several smaller burning logs.

"We have central heating, but don't use it," Bo says. "We do burn the fireplace every day."

We are in an open kitchen area with counters covered in colored Mexican tiles. On one end of the kitchen is a large family room with comfortable over-stuffed couches in pink and mauve. Eating from a bowl on a tile countertop is a beautiful cat with powder-puff fur that blends with the sofa coverings. "We call her She," Bo says as I pet the animal's soft, warm coat.

At the other end of the open kitchen is another room with a long rough-hewn table next to the fireplace. Just outside the window a curtain of water falls from the red-tile roof into a black solar swimming pool. "We recycle the water from the pool to the roof," John says, poking at the blazing logs. "Makes a unique waterfall."

Bo sets a pot of tea and cookies on the table. As I sit down she pours the tea then pulls out a leather-bound photo album and opens it. Inside are color photographs of the *rejoneador* (fighting on horseback) bullfight sequence from the movie *Bolero*.

"This was the most exciting horse to ride," Bo says, pointing at a black stallion. "He was the wildest of all."

Looking at the bull in the photos (actually a large calf), I ask how she learned to ride like a Spaniard in the *rejoneador* fight sequences.

"John," she says. "He taught me how to have a light hand and a good seat, to ride like a Spaniard as if I was part of the horse." She looks at another photo of her riding an agitated palomino past the horns of the calf. "For the fight sequences we used some of the most famous horses in Spain, which we got from the Peralta brothers, the great *rejoneadores*."

Was filming the fight terrifying? I ask. The calf looked big, although it did have leather-covered horns.

"No, I was too excited," she says turning a page of the album. "We went to Spain six weeks early to train so I could get accustomed to the horses before going into the ring with the calf. Unfortunately, I only had three days to train. Then I watched the Peraltas in actual bullfights. When it was time to film, I went in the ring and did it—the first time!" She laughs, eyes bright and proud. "Everybody was shocked, me, John—the Peraltas most of all. They told me I rode like a Spaniard."

John moves away from the fireplace and says, "We were going to take three days to shoot the sequence, but we only had half a day. When Bo got in the ring she was high as a kite with excitement."

You like bullfights? I ask John.

"He studied to be a bullfighter for three years," Bo says quickly.

"You have to be involved with the macho," says John. "It was something I was at the time. I hated acting, thought it was very sissified." (Because of his boyish good looks Derek was condemned to play pretty-boy romantic leads in such movies of the 1950s as *Rogues of Sherwood Forest*. His best-known acting success was as an accused killer opposite Humphrey Bogart in *Knock on Any Door*.)

"Bullfighting does not have to be dangerous," John continues. "It's when your ego gets in the way; that makes it dangerous. The crowd starts pushing you and because you are sick of them, you say to hell with it and get your ass clobbered."

Bo laughs. "It's a good thing John didn't get into the bullfighting ring. His ego would have gotten him killed."

"Ego is a terrible thing," Derek admits.

No one speaks for a moment. I look at the bullfighting photographs. John goes back to the fireplace, pokes the logs a couple times, then leaves Bo and me alone to finish the interview, saying, "You and Bo talk. She has got plenty to say on her own."

As he leaves I ask Bo what she and her husband do when not training and breeding horses.

"We travel a lot," she answers. "We have several projects we are thinking about filming. We may be wrong, but we're not in any hurry." She crosses her legs under her in the chair, curling into a feline position. "We don't have to leave home to work, nor do we have an entourage of agents, managers and lawyers. We do it all ourselves, and produce our own movies. The *Tarzan* movie was commercially very successful, as was *Bolero*.

"Unfortunately, *Bolero* was completely misunderstood by the critics and most of the audience. The ad campaign by the movie company portrayed the film as a *serious* picture. We were making an erotic, sensual, silly, *fun* picture. It was just camp, a corny romance."

She leans forward and her features take on a harder line. "I haven't done anything in any of my movies that I feel bad about. Besides, I would rather use myself as a commodity and exploit myself rather than have someone else do it. What most producers don't realize is they are not exploiting a product, they are exploiting a person. That's dangerous."

And you feel you would have been exploited had you made movies for other producers?

"Oh yes! Absolutely. I am a very strong person, but I was not so strong in the beginning of my career that I couldn't have been used. Believe me, the movie industry can be rotten and miserable and you meet rotten people."

You have taken a lot of severe criticism from the press and movie critics, I say. Does it hurt?

"When I walk down the street people are really friendly," she says slowly, "and I wonder how they can be so nice with all the horrible things that have been written about us. We have done several television interviews here at the ranch to show people *us,* how we really are."

Why do you feel the press treated you this way?

"There is always someone they are attacking, someone they have put on their 'hit' list."

How did you make the list?

She curls herself tighter in the chair. "It began with *Life* magazine. *Life* was looking for a new girl to discover, like they had done with Marilyn Monroe. Producers, as a matter of habit, send movies of their new actresses to *Life* for consideration. Orion Pictures, who had just made *10*, but hadn't released it, sent it in. *Life* picked me as their new discovery."

She unfolds herself and stands up. "*Life* wanted me on the cover coming out of a burlap sack, naked, with a bow in my hair!" She raises her arms over her head illustrating the "popping out of a sack" idea. "Inside the magazine I was supposed to pose for look-alike pictures of Rita Hayworth and Farrah Fawcett. I was to be '*Life*'s Gift to America.' I didn't think of myself as *Life*'s discovery or as their personal present to America, so I said no, thank you."

She plops down on the chair. "That made *Life* furious. I got an immediate call to meet with five of Orion Pictures' top honchos. They couldn't understand why I wouldn't pose for the cover. You would have thought these guys had better things to do than badger one little girl.

"They kept using the old cliché: 'You'll never work in this town again,' but that didn't bother me. I wouldn't be in the movie business or any business and do things against my will. That they couldn't understand.

"I had already signed to do my second movie, *A Change of Seasons* with Shirley MacLaine and Anthony Hopkins. Well, the Orion people called the movie's producer, Marty Ransohoff, and tried to get him to take me off the film. Marty was also a rebel and wouldn't do it, so the editor of *Life* called him and tried to get me canned. Imagine, the editor of *Life*!

"They weren't used to anyone, especially a young actress, saying no. It was so strange to them. Once you say no, that makes them even more determined to get you to say yes. *Life* magazine called me again and said they'd take whatever photos I wanted. I said I'd do beach shots, so they sent over a photographer. *He came with the burlap sack* and an order to shoot the look-alike poses. Again I said no." She sighs. "That's how I got on the 'hit' list."

Even without the cover of *Life* magazine, Bo Derek became a cinematic sensation. The press clamored for information about this new girl who had made the number 10 synonymous with beauty. Orion Pictures, who hadn't dreamed of the impact the movie would make, didn't have a personal biography on Bo. To have something to write about, editors dug out information on John Derek.

"It was all so silly," Bo says. "They found stuff about John being a Svengali, and how he had made Ursula and Linda famous. That press stuff just wasn't true. Ursula and Linda made it on their own. But the writers figured that John was a Pygmalion and that I was his next creation. They termed him a hypnotist, a black magician, a sinister Svengali."

Yet, you wouldn't be where you are today without John, I comment.

"That's true," she answers. "I'd still be a beach bum named Mary Cathleen."

Mary Cathleen Collins met John Derek in 1974 when she was an eighteen-year-old fledgling actress auditioning for a low-budget film *And Once Upon a Time* that Derek was directing on the Greek island of Mykonos. (The picture was released in 1981 under the title *Fantasies*.)

Bo had not seriously thought about being an actress until she met John. She had no theatrical training, and her only link to the movies was from her mother who was a Hollywood hairdresser with clients such as Ann-Margret. Bo was backstage with her mother in Las Vegas when an agent spotted her and said, "You should be in pictures."

She did a couple of television commercials and a little modeling, then was cast as the female lead in the remake of *King Kong*. She turned it down. "I went home and read the script and it was a bunch of dirty jokes about the incompatibility of size, you know, really tacky stuff, so I said, no, thank you. Jessica Lange did it and the script was changed for her." Then John Derek came along.

"Soon after we met, we hated each other," Bo says. "He kept picking on me, saying I was lazy. I thought he was mean. But he was right, I was terribly lazy, which was hurting the film. I wanted to be on the beach.

"I never did feel like Mary Cathleen. I wasn't a Cathy. John started throwing names at me, and I responded to 'Bo.' I knew it was right and used the stage name Bo Shane. John, along with his wife, Linda Evans, who was with him during the filming, discouraged my phony smiles, scrubbed my face clean from the awful makeup I was wearing—I thought it was sophisticated—then took some photographs."

When Bo saw the photographs, she saw someone else, someone not just pretty—which she had been told she was—but someone beautiful, which she didn't realize. John Derek had introduced Bo to herself. When Linda Evans left Greece, John and Bo started living together. The situation was not easy for Linda, and she divorced John, who then, in 1977, married Bo.

On a scale of one to ten, how do you rate John as a husband? I ask.

"For me he's great," she answers.

Any faults?

"No." Bo pauses. "Well . . . he is very opinionated. And . . . sometimes he's hard to live with. He wants things done now; he has no patience. Most of all he can't understand carelessness. I can be careless and do silly things and that doesn't compute in his brain. One of the things that bothers John is that I never contemplate who I am. For me to think about myself is a waste of time. I'm not interested in wondering about the future or why we were placed on earth."

She walks to the window and silently looks out at the rolling hills beyond. Then she says, "I don't need to know what will happen. I've got it all here."

She turns. "And I love it."

John Travolta

Look Who's Talking, Too

"The one-sidedness of an interview is a bit of a drag.
To keep it interesting for myself, I need to ask
questions. Besides, after almost twenty years talking
about myself, I've run out of new things to say."

JOHN TRAVOLTA has just been seated at the restaurant table
when a young man rushes up and thrusts a linen napkin into his
hands. "Uh . . . would . . . you mind autographing this," he stammers with the self-conscious look that the in-the-flesh screen idol
inspires. "Uh . . . it's for Leslie, she's"—he points to another table halfway across the dimly-lighted dining room—"over there."

Travolta smiles and pats the pockets of his trendy, box-shouldered
gray suit. "I don't have a pen," he says.

The young man looks around frantically for a pen to materialize.
Sitting next to Travolta, I pull a felt-tip out of my pocket and hand it to
the actor, who inscribes the napkin, "To Leslie," and autographs it. The
film fan carefully folds the cherished souvenir, mumbles "Thanks," then
adds, "She's going to *love* this," and backpedals past a waiter toward his
table.

He calls back, "We need to see more of you!"

"Oh, you will," Travolta answers, switching on his high-voltage smile. "You're going to see much more of me."

For John Travolta film fans—those thirty- to forty-year-olds who have fed on the hopes and dreams that the actor's celluloid image inspires—that is good news. In the late 1970s and early 1980s Travolta was the on-screen embodiment of the American dream. His swaggering, boogie-ing, all sex-and-energy style mesmerized the "me" generation with his portrayal of "sweathog" Vinnie Barbarino in "Welcome Back, Kotter," the 1975 television series that rocketed his star aloft. Then came 1977 and the phenomenal success of *Saturday Night Fever*, followed by the hit musical *Grease*. His succeeding successes in *Urban Cowboy* and *Staying Alive* kept his star shining.

Travolta's 1985 movie, *Perfect*, was a clinker that disappointed fans and critics alike. The actor thought the film was good and was confused why it didn't appeal to the moviegoer. At the time he grumbled: "*Perfect* was probably better than everyone thought. Yet, because of the bad reviews, I thought I might not want my career to happen anymore. It's humbling being on the planet earth: You win, you lose, you get compliments, you get an insult . . . that's the way it is."

Most actors await reviews with trepidation and Travolta has been no exception. After *Perfect*'s imperfect reception, followed by a 1987 version of Pinter's *The Dumb Waiter*, which passed largely unnoticed on ABC, then *The Expert*, a turgid comedy that was immediately packed off to the video stores, Travolta stopped making films. He put on weight. Hollywood writers mocked his interest in the cultish Church of Scientology. His sexuality was questioned: the tabloids printed rumors that he was gay.

"You get used to what is being said," he says. "You wish that it wasn't there, but you accept yellow journalism as part of an actor's life."

Knowing he would be asked things by the press that would upset him and hurt his work, he made the decision not to see or talk to anyone for a while. Then came the 1989 movie, *Look Who's Talking*, and Travolta was back in action again.

•

Travolta agreed to an interview, stating he preferred that the session be in a restaurant after finishing a day's filming, so he could relax and "just talk, exchange some ideas, have a conversation."

It was 9:30 in the evening when Travolta walked into the 72 Market restaurant—a classy look-for-the-movie-stars eatery near the beach in Venice—for our scheduled "conversation." As Travolta sauntered past the tables, several groups of people froze, then, as if a still-life painting had been brought to life, began to whisper in suppressed excitement. Travolta continued to the corner table, his table, accustomed to the stares. As he sat down, a pianist at a nearby grand piano played selections from the Broadway musical *Grease*.

After the film fan left with the signed napkin, I ask the actor if he minds giving autographs—especially in public places.

"When the request is warm and sincere like that young man's, I really enjoy it," he says. "It's only a bother when it's rude."

I mention the oft-told story about Paul Newman who was asked for an autograph in a men's room—while standing at the urinal, and Travolta laughs: "I heard it was Frank Sinatra."

Travolta picks up a menu and runs his fingers across the rich texture of the cover before opening it to study the selections. One has the feeling that this handsome, stylish actor, who turned forty in 1994, wants to be as warm and sincere as his obligations as a star can allow him to be. Unfortunately, he has been burnt too many times by a probing press and has learned to be cautious. In the past he has had the tendency to say things nakedly that a more cautious actor might say more subtly—or not at all. Yet, he says he likes "revealing himself," adding for the skeptically-minded, "I really do. People who say I'm hard to get to know don't know me. I don't think I'm mysterious."

Having decided on a salad and a pasta entrée, Travolta smiles that big toothy smile, letting the image he projects on the screen shine through. "With no exaggeration," he says, "maybe I've done thousands and thousands of interviews and I've seen most of the approaches; the way a journalist seduces an interviewee. After a while I'd rather just have a good conversation with someone." He pushes the menu aside and leans in, arms on the table, "Look, if I'm going to give a person two hours of my life, I'd rather learn something, exchange some ideas. It would make it more interesting for me. The one-sidedness of an interview is a bit of a drag. To keep it interesting for myself, I need to ask questions. Besides, after almost twenty years of talking about myself, I've run out of new things to say."

He takes a deep breath, and I ask if he tries to think up bright, new quotes before an interview.

"Sure. I wonder what in the hell I have to do to give a good story; be creative, think of a new angle."

I ask about his recent marriage to actress Kelly Preston whom he met in 1987 while filming the bomb, *The Experts*.

"I liked her immediately," he says. "I liked her even better when I found out she loved to travel and didn't mind flying. She was open-minded toward Scientology. She was so refreshing that I thought, 'Wow! She is fun.' But she was married to actor Kevin Gage and I thought, 'Well, too bad.'"

Three years later, when Travolta was in Vancouver filming *Look Who's Talking Too,* he bumped into Kelly again. She had divorced. Travolta and Preston were married in 1992, and nine months later—"I guess Kelly got pregnant the first day we tried"—Travolta came into fatherhood. A baby boy, Jett, named after the planes he loves to fly, was born when Travolta was thirty-eight. "I was ready to be married and have a family when I was fourteen," he says.

Why *didn't* you marry earlier? I ask.

"I was almost married three times," he answers softly. (His first love, actress Diana Hyland, who was eighteen years older, died in his arms, a victim of cancer in 1977. After her death, he was linked with several women, including Marilu Henner.)

"By the third time I began to realize I didn't marry because I didn't *want* to be." He pauses, then continues cautiously. "Two of the women I considered were famous and I didn't want to mention their names because in all fairness they eventually married and are now very happy."

The pianist ripples off a swing tune as Travolta continues. "Look, I understand what makes a good interview and I used to talk about all the women I went with. And then I got a couple phone calls that said in essence, 'Please shut up, John!'

"I think the real reason to marry is to have children. You can have a relationship with a woman and you don't have to get married—you know what I mean?" His voice takes on a serious tone. "I think having children is a lovely reason to get married, a valid one. And that's the way I feel." He leans back in his chair. "You know, Jimmy Stewart didn't get married until he was forty-one, and then had children."

The waiter arrives to take our order. At this late hour the surge of early diners are gone and half the restaurant's tables are now empty. After the waiter leaves, I ask Travolta if he ever met Jimmy Stewart.

"No, but he's the only one I haven't."

When Travolta uses the word *one*, his voice is tinged with reverence. He has long made a point of seeking out the great actors he admires. "We're all fans," he says.

"I met Cary Grant, and I knew Jimmy Cagney really well—we became friends—and I know Kirk Douglas, and I've met Gregory Peck, but of the older guys, Jimmy Stewart's the only one I've admired that I haven't met.

"I've always felt something special for the great stars," he continues. "Now that I've had the opportunity to meet them, why not take advantage of it. Look, I don't know what it's like to have been a legend for forty years. Why not learn from them? But more than that, why not simply enjoy having a conversation with someone you've respected for so long."

Travolta pauses as the waiter slides a lettuce salad in front of the actor. "When I began, my biggest supporter was Fred Astaire. He told me that he felt my dancing was an extension of a lot of the things he had created in dance. After seeing *Saturday Night Fever*, he asked me,

'Where did you learn that walk? That was exciting; the way you just walked down the street.' This from Astaire," Travolta says.

"I was awe struck. He had so many wonderful things to say; he was a real gentleman."

Travolta is quiet, thinking, perhaps, about those few cherished moments with Astaire. Then he says, "I don't know why *Saturday Night Fever* worked. We thought we were doing a little slice-of-life film using the black and Hispanic influence. We had no idea it was going to be a blockbuster movie."

Because of *Saturday Night Fever*, Travolta was, at age twenty-four, one of the hottest pieces of property on the cinematic scene, and to his fans, the personification of the American Dream. But, then, he always figured he would be.

"I've known since I was nineteen that I wanted success," he says. "I'm goal-oriented and having success is important to me. I don't think I would have been happy without it. In fact, I know I would have been quite miserable."

Born in Englewood, New Jersey, in 1954, the youngest of six children (his brother, Joey, tried show business as did his sisters, Ellen and Margaret), Travolta remembers that acting came naturally to him. His mother, Helen (who died in 1978), kept busy with local theater activities and instilled the love of greasepaint in her children. Against his father's advice, Travolta dropped out of school at age sixteen to try an acting career. While playing the lead in a New Jersey stage production of *Bye Bye Birdie*, he was spotted by an agent who got him work doing commercials. Deciding that he could make a name for himself on the West Coast, Travolta packed his bags and headed for Hollywood.

Not long after his arrival in the film capital, the handsome, six-foot tall, 170-pound actor auditioned for the part of the swaggering, posturing Vinnie Barbarino in "Welcome Back, Kotter," and was picked from a crowd of a hundred other young actors for the part. He made his first impact on feature movie audiences with his supporting role in *Carrie*. These early successes led to the starring role in *Saturday Night Fever*.

For his portrayal of Tony Manero, a young man trying to escape his dreary existence by way of disco dancing, Travolta was nominated for a Best Actor Academy Award.

"If someone had told me when we were filming *Saturday Night Fever* that I was going to get an Oscar nomination, I would have told them they were crazy." He raises his right hand like he is taking an oath. "I swear to God. It was like a dream. I had just returned from Mexico on a week holiday and when I was told at the airport that I had been nominated, my life went into slow motion for five minutes. I jumped in the air—and never came down. I dove full-length into the open door of this waiting limo, and I was *still* in slow motion." He laughs. "The silliest thing was I was in this car by myself and there was no one to celebrate with."

After the waiter sets the entrées in front of us, I ask if it was a disappointment when he lost the Oscar.

"Absolutely not! Here you are, twenty-four years old and you've been nominated for a picture you never considered would be that great, and you think, well, you'll get the Oscar at age forty or fifty, so the idea of winning is really far out. My mother, who I took to the award ceremony along with my father, didn't hear the name of the winning actor when the announcement was made. She asked, 'Did you win?' My father answered, 'No.' She said, 'Good.' I asked her why she said that, and she replied, 'Now, you'll have something to look forward to.'"

Although Travolta didn't win the Oscar that year (Richard Dreyfuss did for *Goodbye Girl*), he would like to be considered again, someday. "I'd like to be in a film where there's a role that would be artistically deserving of an award, like where I started in *Fever*.

"My goal is to continue to act, to sing, to dance for the rest of my life," he continues. "I did a movie where I danced, then I did a pure drama, and a pure comedy. Because I'm able to do all of those things, I have it better than anyone else in the industry."

One of the best times was with the 1989 release of *Look Who's Talking*, the film that centered on Mikey, a cynical, wise-cracking baby determined to find himself a father. The successful movie co-starred Kirstie Alley as the unwed mother, Travolta as the kid's number-one choice for Da-da, and Bruce Willis as the voice of the miniature matchmaker Mikey. After the movie earned $46 million in its first seventeen days of release, Hollywood insiders were once again saying nice things about Travolta.

Amy Hecklering, who wrote the movie with Travolta in mind said, "John has proved he's a wonderful actor with good comic timing, and he's sexy. What else do you need from a guy?"

The producers felt differently and decided to soft-pedal Travolta's presence in the movie, saying that they didn't worry that his name would keep people away, but they were also not sure it would be a big draw. "It wouldn't be fair to sell the movie as a John Travolta Film," one producer was quoted as saying. "When you have an actor whose past few movies didn't do well, you have to stop and think. And we wanted to sell a comedy."

Travolta says he liked his work in the movie and went along with the marketing strategy. "I didn't want the release to be blown," he says. "I wanted this movie to be good. Really good. Good enough so people would look up to me again and say, 'There goes an actor.'"

Travolta agreed to make *Look Who's Talking Too,* and after its success signed on for *Look Who's Talking III.* The actor has turned down other work saying he's too involved in "Bringing Up Baby—Part I."

Travolta orders coffee from the waiter and begins to query me on whom I have interviewed, whom I have enjoyed interviewing, carrying on the "conversation" that he says he enjoys. One can see that he is a little uncomfortable and nervous talking about himself. He asks me if I have any interest in Scientology, noting how much his own belief has relieved him from stress since he became interested in it in 1975. "Scientology is quite the opposite of what shrinks do," he says. "It's more of a science than a theory; the nuts and bolts of self-help." He advises that he is a trained "auditor" and has helped many people—"I can adjust injuries or the emotional losses of others. It has its spiritual aspects"—then offers to audit me. "Sure, during a lunch hour, sometime," he says, eyes bright. "I'm serious. Scientology has techniques that get you through life. If you need help, I'm there."

Our conversation is interrupted when the young man who asked for the autograph comes up to the table leading a self-conscious "Leslie" by the hand. She develops lockjaw when her screen idol in-the-flesh gives her a warm, winning smile and shakes her hand. She leaves, caressing the warmth on her fingers.

Travolta looks at me happily and grins. He may not be an Oscar winner, but, perhaps, that will come. For now, he knows one thing—he's an actor—and a father. He's feeling fine. In control.

And the feeling is good.

Ann Jillian
Through the Looking Glass

"In the movie scene where I was given the injection, I would taste the metal in my mouth again and feel the burning sensation and the fuzziness—then the sickness. And the anger would come back to me, all the hate I had toward this thing called cancer."

SHE was beautiful and she had on a lot of makeup, and the hotel's security director—a moonlighting Chicago police sergeant named Andy Murcia—figured her for either a lady of the evening or a theatrical type. The cop, responsible for keeping pimps, hookers, and burglars away from Chicago's Ambassador East Hotel, followed the woman across the lobby and into the Pump Room. The maître d' asked her if she wanted to sit at a table or at the bar.

Before she could answer, the cop said, "Let her sit at the bar and I'll ask her to dance."

The woman walked away; then turned, looked back over her shoulder at the cop and said with a smile, "I'm going to take a table, then you can come over and ask me to dance."

Ann Jillian laughs, with the deep, throaty laugh of the gum-chewing, brassy Cassie on the television comedy series "It's a Living." "I have always been proud of that scene," she says. "That's the way Andy and I really met in Chicago, and that's the way the scene was played in my movie. I lived a script long before it became one."

"I think she's *always* living a script," her husband, Andy Murcia, says happily. "Even before she made the movie, her life was scripted out for her."

Ann Jillian and her husband are sitting in the living room of their unpretentious but comfortable Los Angeles home—she calls it their "Ozzie-and-Harriet house"—talking about their made-for-television movie, *The Ann Jillian Story*. The film chronicled Ann and Andy's personal love story, but even more, Ann's deeply moving and inspiring ordeal with breast cancer. The critically well-received film drew a large viewing audience to become the highest-rated original television movie of the 1987–88 season. It also made Ann Jillian a symbol of hope for millions of women who suffer from breast cancer.

Ann played herself in the movie. "That movie—in one nutshell statement—was the most difficult thing I ever had to do," Ann says, then adds, "and it always will be."

It isn't easy for an actress to portray her own persona. It has the elements of a play by Pirandello; the actress becomes a mirror image of herself, an illusion that is at once real and fantastical. It's like Alice stepping through the looking glass into another world.

"It was an unusual situation," Ann Jillian says, relaxing into an overstuffed couch. She is flawlessly made-up; her skin at age thirty-eight is smooth and unlined, and her platinum hair curves around her head like a white plume. Her dress is casual: a soft pink sweater, brown corduroy slacks, and pink and green argyle socks.

"When the filming first began," she continues, "I kept asking myself, 'How would *she* do this?' . . . then, 'What would *I* do?' Between 'How would she do this?' and 'What would I actually do as the actress,' I'd end up laughing at myself. I was the actress and the real person all at one time.

"When I had to think back to the time when Andy"—she looks at her husband who is standing behind the opposite couch—"and I first met in the hotel in Chicago, I saw the scene in the third person. I remembered *another* young woman, and not me, even though I knew intellectually it was me." She cocks her head quizzically. "Does that make sense?"

She stretches her long legs (she is five-feet eight-inches) under the glass-topped coffee table. "Sometimes it was very difficult. When we were filming, I'd say to myself, that's how it felt, and that's how it was, but you know what's really bothering me?" She looks up at the ceiling, stretches her arms wide and cries, *"The whole building we're filming the scene in is bothering me!"*

The movie was filmed in Toronto, Canada, not Chicago, New York, or Los Angeles where the actual story took place. Scenes could be re-created, but could not be duplicated, creating a difficulty for Ann—and Andy.

"I went to Chicago on my own with a camera and took pictures of all the landmarks and places where we went, what we did," Andy says, "and I asked the producers to please use Chicago. How do you duplicate those little things? The restaurant and coffee shop we went to . . ."

In *The Ann Jillian Story,* Andy Murcia was portrayed by Tony Lo Bianco, an Italian with sharp, dark features and a slender frame. Murcia is Irish and Spanish and his skin is pale, his features rounded.

"Nobody knows what I look like," Andy says, easing onto the couch next to his wife, and folding his arms over his ample stomach. He is a warm, friendly, good-natured huggy-bear of a man with a gruff edge—a characteristic, no doubt, left over from his days as a Chicago cop.

Ann Jillian studies her husband for a moment. "To me Andy has an Irish look. He has the map of Ireland all over his face."

Were the two of them pleased with the movie?

"Yes," Ann answers quickly. "Everybody at NBC was wonderful, and working with the director, Cory Allen, was great. I loved what he did. There is no way I could have had a screaming director. I would have been in my dressing room saying, 'Okay, when you're calm and civil, I'll come out.'"

Andy responds slowly to the question. "I'm real picky." His brow furrows; then shaking his head, he adds, "I've got a problem with this movie, and I've been trying to put my feelings together."

He pauses, thinking it out before saying it: "I'm *jealous* of the guy, Tony, who played me."

He leans forward, trying to explain, using his hands: "Not mad at him—jealous. Because next to me *he knows my wife almost as intimately as I do*. I think I resent that and it makes it hard for me to look at this thing objectively. I went through this cancer ordeal with her. She's *my girl*." He shakes his head. "I wish to hell I would have been an actor and done it myself."

Ann smiles warmly at him. There is obviously a lot of love between the two of them.

Their close family ties are evident in the living room: the fireplace mantel is lined with family snapshots; a table near the front window also has a profusion of framed family pictures, as does a baby grand piano. On the glass-topped coffee table are photo envelopes stuffed with new family pictures waiting to be sorted and framed.

Andy shuffles a few of these photographs. "Don't get me wrong. I think Tony Lo Bianco did a great job. He would come to Ann's trailer before a scene, and he would say, 'Andy, make it naked for me, I want your guts! Strip it for me, come on babe.'" Andy wipes his hand across his mouth. "He would get me to a point where I was almost reliving it again. He would say, 'What did you do to her when she was sick from chemotherapy? What did you do with your hands?' And I said I was rubbing her back, like in a circle motion—she was over the toilet—I was holding her poor little stomach." He stops suddenly and looks over at Ann and sees something in her face. "Am I saying something wrong?" he asks.

"No, you're not," she says softly.

The experience of reliving the discovery of her cancer, the removal of both breasts, and the four months of chemotherapy was more traumatic than she had anticipated.

"I thought I would be protected because of the time that had passed, and because I could attack it from an actress's point of view. But it wasn't that easy," she says.

The hardest thing for Ann Jillian was reliving chemotherapy. "In the movie scene where I was given the injection, I would taste the metal in my mouth again and feel the burning sensation and the fuzziness—then the sickness. And the anger would come back to me, all the hate I had toward this thing called cancer."

Why did Ann Jillian subject herself to the ordeal again? Was it the actress in her trying to get out? Or was it something more? When she was still in the hospital recovering from her double mastectomy, a studio literary agent called and said, "Don't worry, we'll get you a book deal."

Ann Jillian's eyes go wide. "'A book deal?' I said, 'Get out of my face; I haven't come out of anesthesia!'"

Ann didn't do the "book deal." But she did go public with her story and her struggle against cancer. "When you have an adversity, you can turn it around and make it work for the good of others," she says. One reason she decided to tell her story was a letter she received from a nun in New York.

"She said it very simply," Ann says, "'God chooses his teachers in strange ways.'"

Ann, whose Catholic faith has always been a cornerstone of her life, told her story in national magazines. The response was startling—she received more than 100,000 letters. Ann started a "Life Saved" file of letters from women who had decided to do something about breast cancer. "I know women were saying, 'If that blonde jumping bean can do it, if she can live through a mastectomy, then so can I.'"

Then NBC suggested making the story into a movie. At first Ann was reluctant to do it. Then she thought: *If a magazine article could help this many people and save lives, think what one night of a movie could do. Millions of people would see it!*

She also felt that the movie would be the final act in talking publicly about her ordeal. She would continue to address the subject on a humanitarian level (she is the spokeswoman for the American Cancer Society), but she would separate that from her work as an actress.

At first Ann didn't think she would play the role of herself in the movie. "She was the only one who thought so," Andy says. "She kept saying, 'No, it shouldn't be me,' and it took three days to convince her."

Although Ann Jillian looks healthy and fit sitting on the couch today, at that time her chemotherapy treatments had caused her to go from a size 8 to a size 16. The fact that she had to portray a size-8, twenty-six-year-old woman in a movie spawned a dieting panic. "I had told the producer I would use some of my own clothes in the film; then I discovered I couldn't put my leg into some of them!" She lost the weight in five months—and has kept it off.

It's tough to squeeze ten years into ninety-four minutes of a movie. Does Ann Jillian feel it was a fair representation of this ever-changing and dramatic period of her life?

"Yes, it was," she says slowly; then hedges, "but there was one thing the movie missed. Andy and I both wanted to have some montages to explain visually, in a capsulated form, what transpired in my career as an actress." She smiles wistfully. "We wanted that so badly."

"The problem was, the movie represented her more as a singer," Andy adds. "Sure that's what she was when she started out, and that's what she was when I met her, but her fame came as the result of her acting and her Emmy nominations for her portrayal of Mae West and her acting job in *Ellis Island*." He shrugs. "Where was that stuff in the film? What does anyone know about her life before we met?"

In 1989 Andy Murcia coauthored with Bob Stewart, a friend whose wife had discovered she had breast cancer the same week as Ann, the book, *Man to Man—When the Woman You Love Has Breast Cancer*, published by St. Martin's Press. It was the first book about breast cancer from the male point of view and sold over 40,000 copies.

Two years later Ann Jillian gave birth to Andrew Joseph H. Nauseda Murcia IV, the first celebrity to beat breast cancer and to go on and have a child. Andy loves to tell the story behind his son's long name:

"Andrew Joseph was my father's name as well as mine. The H. initial is from tough Chicago music critic, Howard Reich, who gave a rave review to Ann's concert at Drury Lane. That night we celebrated with Mexican food and margaritas, and . . . well, Ann's doctor pinpointed that as the time she conceived.

"Nauseda is Ann's real name," Andy adds.

Jurate Nauseda was the second child born to Lithuanian parents. Ann's mother wanted to be an actress, but had to leave Lithuania in 1945 to escape the Russian takeover. "I was born in Cambridge, Massachusetts," Ann says, "but I must have been conceived on the USS *General Mercy* enroute to America!" And she bursts into laughter.

Her mother had little Jurate dancing and singing by the time she was four years old. The little girl appeared on Art Linkletter's television program, "House Party," and was asked to sing. She did, and they practically had to get the hook to get her offstage. When she was twelve, she auditioned for the film *Gypsy* and got the part of Dainty June opposite Natalie Wood and Rosalind Russell. Ann also played Little Bo Peep in Walt Disney's classic, *Babes In Toyland*. She continued performing through high school and later obtained a scholarship to the Los Angeles Civic Light Opera.

While performing as a torch singer with a traveling troupe, Ann met Chicago police sergeant Andy Murcia. She quit performing to dedicate her time to being a wife.

"There I was, a policeman's wife with no place for the creativity to get out," she recalls. "It was trying to come out my fingers, out of my pores." That's when she met Mickey Rooney and was cast with him and Ann Miller in the Broadway smash hit, *Sugar Babies*. An executive from NBC saw the show and cast her as Cassie in the television comedy series "It's a Living."

Another blonde bombshell had landed in Hollywood.

"Hey, that's not a bad ticket in!" she says. "After all, Hollywood is considered a *pretty* industry, and if they consider you to be in that arena, it's flattering. Did I think I was being thought of as strictly a body and nothing else? Quite possibly. But the people who looked beyond it knew the *body* was doing some good stuff. The *body* was doing comedy and the *body* was doing drama, and to tell the truth"—she slaps her hips—"this body never considered herself to be the best body in Hollywood."

Although Ann Jillian was asked, she never played nude scenes. Today, even the sexy stuff is not a thing of the past for Ann. She can't show cleavage, of course, but she can look great in a sweater. (Since her chest muscles are intact, she could have reconstructive surgery, but instead, she wears prostheses—and can order them to any size. With her sense of humor, Ann finds it easier to laugh at this than cry.)

Before she had her mastectomy, Ann played the sexiest—and her personal favorite—role of her career: Mae West. On a wall in her living room is a near-life-size photograph of Ann in a tight-waisted black gown and feathered hat. She looks at the photograph and says, "Mae West was a flamboyant and wonderful character, and she gave me my acting stripes." (Ann's career includes Emmy nominations for her performance in *Ellis Island* [1984], and *Mae West* [1982], in which she also received a Golden Globe nomination. She lost both the Emmy and Golden Globe to Ingrid Bergman who won for *Golda*. "I consider it a personal career high to come in second to Ingrid Bergman any day," Ann says. She did win the Golden Globe Award for Best Actress for *The Ann Jillian Story*.)

In the Mae West story, Ann didn't try to mimic the voice or mannerisms of the "Come up and see me sometime" actress; she tried to capture the essence of the actress. "My knees went weak right after I finished the movie," she says. "It was in the can, and now"—she puts her hands over her eyes then raises her arms over her head in a gesture of supplication—"and now . . . *ay yi yi!* What are people going to think about it? And who is this pseudo-Mae West who came from a television sitcom?"

She needn't have worried. True, for the first five minutes the audience was aware that it was an actress playing Mae West—and then they forgot. Ann Jillian was not just a torch singer, or a comedian spouting one-liners—she was an actress.

Ann continues to act in television movies and mini-series. In 1993 she starred in *Labor of Love,* a true story, and *Little White Lies,* a romantic comedy costarring Tim Matheson. Recently released was the February 1994 movie-of-the-week, *McShanes Grand Slam,"* with Kenny Rodgers, and another true story aired later in the year titled *Heart of a Child.*

She stretches her arms, tiring from the long interview. And you have to look at her, this sometime blonde bombshell, with the unbridled exuberance, and the lively eyes, and the platinum hair and flawless complexion, and think that she can accomplish anything she wants. This attitude fits in with her answer when asked how would she like to be remembered fifty years from now.

She pauses for a few moments and then says softly, "Just say that Ann Jillian made somebody feel good, made somebody smile."

Sharon Stone

Stone Goddess

"If you're going to be bad on screen, then be bad.
Don't go, Wink, wink, wink: 'I'm really good at
home.' Go, 'I'm bad and this is what's going to
happen to you, fool.'"

"**M**IDNIGHT." *Her voice was deep, sensual.
"After I'm finished filming."*
"I'll be there."
*I started to hang up the receiver, then I heard her faraway voice:
"Don't you want to know where?"*
"Where?"
"My room."
*Right. She told me the hotel-suite number: I wrote it in ball-point on
the palm of my hand. At the stroke of midnight I rapped lightly on the
door.*
I tapped again. Then the voice: "Come in."
*Sharon was stretched languidly on a white sofa. She had just come
from the shower wrapped in a white terry-cloth robe, her blond hair still
wet. No makeup, just a little baby oil on her face, that smooth lineless
face. The eyes, even without the on-camera highlighting, were intense,*

*penetrating, the eyebrows naturally dark. I noted the toenails, scarlet
against the white . . .*

No, that's not what happened.

Truth is, she plopped onto the couch wearing a baggy blue sweater, a
gray, ankle-length skirt, and heavy blue socks. She was far from steamy
and smoldering. Her eyes were tired from the day's shooting: crisp lines
darting from the corners. Yet, she made the best of the late hour and
was forthright and funny, a goddess in gray and blue.

How have you achieved what you have today? I asked, noting that
her per-film fees have skyrocketed since *Basic Instinct,* the movie that
catapulted her onto a pedestal above Hollywood's glamour goddesses. It
grossed $116 million. Stone now commands fees in the neighborhood of
$4 million a movie.

"I've learned to get what I want by being direct and fearless," Stone
responded. "I'm not a sucking-up type of person." She smiled wickedly,
and added, "If you have a vagina and a point of view, that's a deadly
combination."

One certainly can't mistake that for an android talking. This take-no-
prisoners stance on life, love, and career helped parlay Stone's talents
into her breakthrough role in *Basic Instinct.* It also took a little luck.

She'd been passed over for lead parts in *Fatal Attraction, Dick Tracy*
and *Batman,* and when director Paul Verhoeven began looking for an
actress to play Catherine Tramell, the bisexual bad girl in *Basic Instinct*,
Sharon Stone wasn't even on his list. She got the role by default: Neither
Michelle Pfeiffer or Julia Roberts wanted it, nor did Geena Davis.
Verhoeven, who had worked with her in 1990 when she portrayed
Arnold Schwarzenegger's wife in *Total Recall* (her only role of any note
up to that point), tested her and was impressed. She had the sexy, steely,
scary on-screen strength he was looking for. Because Michael Douglas
was reluctant to have her do the part (he said he wanted an actress with
"more of an equal stature"), they kept her waiting for five months. Some
of the equal-stature ladies didn't want to do nudity; others had taken off

their clothes too often. Sharon Stone was ready for a really good part and when she got it—as Michael Douglas said—"She really kicked ass."

Sharon bent one leg, showing the line of her thigh as the robe parted, and I savored the memory of her un-ladylike uncrossing of her legs in Basic Instinct . . .

Sharon Stone's portrayal in *Basic Instinct* was hailed by critics as one of the great performances by a woman in screen history. The scene in the police station interrogation room showed a fully sexual woman turning tough cops to jelly with the curl of a smile and a twist of the hips. In a flash of cinematic brilliance, she silenced a room of lusty police investigators by merely uncrossing her legs. She was, the reviewers agreed, fabulous.

"Catherine Tramell *was* big and fabulous," Stone said, sinking deeper into the sofa, becoming part of the soft pillows. "But you want to know something? I ain't her. Smart people know I'm not her, but even smarter people know I can be her if I need to be."

A scene from *Basic Instinct* flashed across my mind, the one of her sensually kissing another woman. You mean, I asked, that you've had sex with another woman?

She smiled mischievously. "A gay woman asked me out on a date, and I've gone out on a date to see . . . 'cause, you know, men can be annoying. So once in a while you hope that—Oh, God!—maybe there could be an alternative. But unfortunately for me there isn't. Because I love women. I love being with girlfriends. God! If I could get into it, it would be great. But you know, it don't mean a thing if it ain't got that *schwing!*" She laughed and happily hugged herself.

Sharon patted the couch next to her, let a slow, beguiling smile steal over her face, and asked if I would like a drink, then poured from a decanter of dark cream sherry . . .

131

"You know, I'm a girl who *really likes boys*," she continued, "and I like a guy who will treat me like a girl. I'm very old-fashioned. Occasionally," she winked, "I *do* wear underwear." Another flash from *Basic Instinct:* Sharon Stone drop-dead chic in her white sheath sans underwear.

"I am for sure a broad," she added, her eyes smiling.

As Sharon handed me the glass of sherry, her fingers brushed against mine . . .

One thing for sure about Sharon Stone—you'd have to be a strong guy to go with her. Otherwise she'd blow you away. A fact that was discovered by her husband, TV producer Michael Greenburg (whom she divorced in 1985), and by her past boyfriends: twenty-four-year old Chris Peters (son of producer Jon Peters and Lesley Ann Warren, and eleven years Stone's junior), and country star Dwight Yoakum. She dropped Yoakum after a six-week affair, noting, "A dirt sandwich is better than Dwight Yokum." Hunky actor Hart Bochner, dismayed when Sharon left, referred to her as "the anti-Christ."

In 1993 Stone attached herself to Bill MacDonald, the executive producer of her poorly received exotic thriller, *Sliver.* MacDonald was a newlywed at the time of the affair, having just married his live-in love of eight years, Naomi, who suffered a miscarriage shortly after. Sharon happily announced, "We're not married, but we're taking a honeymoon anyway," a revelation that caused Naomi's mother to refer to Stone as "Slut Sharon."

I sipped from the glass of sherry, my eyes, over the rim of the glass, deep into hers . . .

The tabloids have had a ball with her who-gives-a-damn sexuality, headlining her excesses: TINSELTOWN'S BIGGEST HEART-BREAKER and HOLLYWOOD'S SEXY REBEL.

"I hang the raunchiest stories on my bulletin board," Stone said, unfazed by it all. "I'm tough and strong. My I.Q. is over 150, and I'll never play dumb for any man, nor will I let any man hurt me or step on me. If people think I'm a bitch, tough!"

This in-your-face approach has not endeared her to everyone. The story goes that she was so disliked on the set of *Allan Quartermaine and the Lost City of Gold* (a 1987 film that quickly went south at the box office) that before her bathing scene, crew members urinated in the water. "So maybe they didn't like me sometimes," she said. "Tough shit!"

Tough lady.

How tough? Sharon bragged to Hollywood writers, "I can get any man I want—and now that I'm famous, I get to torture a higher class of man than I used to!"

After our first drink, the couch seemed to get smaller. I could smell Sharon's perfume, the scent of a goddess. I eased closer . . .

Sure, her off-the-cuff quotes bite hard, but Sharon Stone's having fun. She feels she deserves it. After all, it took her a long time to reach her present plateau of power.

Referring to her new celebrity, she said, "I earned this. I didn't come out here and say I was the greatest actress in the world right out of the chute. Sometimes I was good; sometimes I was really stinky. They didn't owe me anything. I stayed. I held my place in line. They got to my number. . . . You have to understand that when I got here I was twenty-one and looked sixteen and had this voice and this attitude. There was nowhere for me. The best slot that people felt that they could put me into was the bimbo slot . . . I looked like a Barbie."

Sharon Stone took her first step up the cinematic staircase when she left home at nineteen to become a model in New York. Later, as her career was rocketing skyward, she posed nude for the July 1990 issue of *Playboy*. Why did she agree to bare it all for *Playboy*? "My greed and avarice," she said. "I was making $500 a day." Stone later posed for the April 1993 cover of *Vanity Fair,* staring little-girl-like into the camera, nude from the waist up, her hands cupping her breasts. "I hate that shot!" she growled.

Sharon curled her arms luxuriously around a pillow, the top of the robe opening to show the curve . . .

Basic Instinct was her eighteenth movie. She trained for all those years by slogging through one minor-league picture after another: *Police Academy 4, Action Jackson, Above the Law,* and *Irreconcilable Differences.* In the 1985 film *King Solomon's Mines,* Stone had the part of an archaeology student in Africa, tracking her kidnapped father. It was all camp, and when a tribe of cannibals dumped Stone and Richard Chamberlain into a pot of simmering vegetables, he gushed, "Did anyone tell you you look ravishing with onions in your hair?" *The Year of the Gun* was a lifeless thriller in which she played a photographer threatened by terrorists, followed by *Scissors,* a 1990 dud with Stone cast as an improbable twenty-six-year-old virgin. She was thirty-three at the time.

With a non-too-steady hand, my fingers traced their way across the silkiness of the sofa fabric . . . reaching . . .

"I guess *Scissors* was my favorite bad movie," Stone said. "In that one I was locked in an apartment alone, furniture bolted down, and for some reason this drives me insane." She brushed a wisp of blond hair away from her forehead. "I know they were terribly stupid movies, but they paid the rent."

Her more recent films paid a lot more rent, such as *Intersection,* in which she played the long-suffering, devoted wife of Richard Gere—"I know, tough," Stone said. She has been scheduled for a *Basic Instinct* sequel.

I asked if she would accept $20 million dollars to do a lousy movie today.

She laughed. "No. They are offering me unmentionable sums of money to do good movies."

My fingers brushed against hers . . .

The weariness began to show in her face, tired lines deepening around the corners of her mouth. "I *really* would like to slip into something more comfortable." She lowered her eyelids, and let out a long sigh. "Like a soft down comforter."

She was tembling, too. Her neck was soft . . . I pulled her closer . . .

So you're a tease.

"Well, not intentionally," she teased, rising slowly, padding toward the bedroom in the gray socks.

Then, as she slipped around the corner of the door like a curl of smoke, she added in her bad-boy voice, "I really am a good little girl—sometimes."

The scene faded to black. All that was left was the scent of her perfume . . .

THE END

Author's note: This interview is pure fantasy; the only illusory interview in the book. But only the questions and the setting and the costumes and the action were made up. Everything Sharon Stone said is real, and on the record—somewhere.

As for the interviewer, he's real, too—at least in his own imagination. He's still on that couch, a writer in search of a character, one with blond hair, blue eyes—and scarlet toenails.

Chris Mitchum

My Father's Footsteps

"People talk about walking in the footsteps of my
father. I see that we're walking on the same beach,
but I'm making my own footprints."

"**I**T WAS my very first day on the set of an Asian movie,
and I was supposed to fight fourteen people. The cameras
were set up in a karate studio, and the director had blocked out all the
karate moves with the stunt people. We did the first take.

"Then there was silence."

Chris Mitchum pauses, his expressive hands still for a moment.
"Finally, the director walked over to me and said, 'It doesn't look like
you're *hitting* them.'"

Mitchum laughs. "I stared at him kind of funny and said, 'Well, they
have to snap their heads back, double over, fake it, not just stand there.'

"'No, I mean, it doesn't look like you're making contact,' the director
tried to explain to me. 'You're supposed to *hit* them. That's what they're
here for.'

"'You mean really kick them, hit them?'"

With an incredulous look on his face, Chris Mitchum folds his arms

137

and leans back in his chair as he tells the story about the first movie he made with Asian film makers. He is sitting in the living room of his home dressed casually in a faded pink tee shirt, jeans, and tennis shoes. In his mid-forties, Mitchum is a lithe, athletic actor, fairer than his father, Robert Mitchum: his hair blond, the eyelashes golden in the rush of the early-morning sun. He bears only a vague resemblance to the elder actor, a fleeting similarity one would have to look closely to find.

And that suits Chris Mitchum just fine.

The second son of Robert Mitchum defiantly points out that he is his own man, making his own career, carving his own path, independently of his famous father.

"I happen to be in the same business," he says, as if he has had to explain his feelings on the subject a thousand times. "But I'm not following in his footsteps and trying to have his career any more than I would try to have Kirk Douglas's or Clint Eastwood's career."

Like Eastwood, Chris Mitchum went to Europe, then Asia, to make films and fashion his acting career. Although he performed in several American films, most notably costarring with John Wayne in *Rio Lobo* and *Big Jake,* and in the mid-1980s with his father and son in the television movie *Promises to Keep,* Mitchum has made a name for himself in foreign movies.

"I have a black belt in karate, and that helped me a lot with the Asian films," he says, returning to his story about the karate fight. "My style is a little harder than that of Chinese Kung Fu, but the director told me to hit the stunt people so I went ahead and did it. I did try to hold back a little, but when you're fighting that many people, and you miss by even a quarter of an inch, you can knock out a tooth or break a rib. I finished the fight scene and there were four guys lying on the floor groaning, holding their faces and sides. The director yelled, 'Cut!' and everybody on the set applauded."

Mitchum holds up his forearms. "I went home the first day and both legs from my knees to my ankles, and my entire forearms, were black and blue from blocking punches to keep from getting waxed."

Mitchum was establishing himself as an action star, not unlike his father, who made a career out of being a macho hero. Chris Mitchum says that his father has given him almost no advice about acting. "I believe he feels people should be independent like he was when he was young, and find their own truths in life."

Making films overseas gave the younger Mitchum the chance to discover the truth and—as he says—"to take the time to find out who I was and build my own personality as well as movie career."

In 1970 he made his first movie in Spain. Then, after a few months back in the United States, the Spanish producers asked him to do a second film. When he returned to Spain he discovered, to his amazement, that the first movie had won several local equivalents to an Academy Award and was the highest-grossing Spanish film in the country's history. "I was suddenly a major motion picture star in Spain," Mitchum says. "People were stopping me on the street, asking for autographs."

Mitchum figured Spain was the place to be and moved his wife, Cynthia, daughter, Carrie, and son, Bentley, to Madrid. They lived there for three years before returning to the United States, settling in Santa Barbara, California, not far from his father and mother's home.

In 1985, Mitchum starred in the American television movie, *Promises To Keep*. The film showcased three generations of Mitchums: Chris, his son Bentley—and Robert Mitchum.

Chris Mitchum felt extremely nervous about doing the picture.

"Sure I was nervous," Mitchum admits, folding one long leg under the other on the sofa chair, "but I was also excited about the project. *Promises* was my first opportunity to work as an actor with my father. Over the years, I have been offered lots of scripts." He assumes the gruff voice of a producer: "'Get your dad to do this and there's a part in it for you . . .'" Mitchum screws up his mouth distastefully. "I'd say, 'Thanks a lot. Call his agent.'"

He looks around the living room of his home, eyes passing over an area hung with large black and white photographs taken by his wife, compositions of rustic walls and windows in Spain and France, full of texture and contrast. Then, still somewhat reluctant to talk about his father, he continues:

"I was nervous because I didn't know how it would be working with my father. If I were filming with another actor like Richard Boone, and he said, 'Well, about this scene, if you did it so and so . . .' I'd say, 'Yeah, but if I were over here . . .' and we'd have an exchange of ideas and reach an understanding how the two of us would play the scene. But when your dad says, 'I think you ought to do this . . .'" Mitchum nods his head dutifully, acting it out: "'Yeah, Dad, sure Dad, sure.'"

Although the actual filming with his father went smoothly, the results were very disappointing to Chris Mitchum.

"I'm sorry we didn't steal the idea and produce it ourselves," he says with a grimace. "We ended up with all this hokey junk, and that's after reading twenty-two scripts written by six different screenwriters. The movie executives only wanted something to fill time between the commercials. What they were selling was the Mitchum, Mitchum, Mitchum package, the publicity angle. They really didn't care about the story."

He leans forward. "We finally went to a meeting with all these big executives and they said what a great show *Promises* would be, and . . ." he pauses thoughtfully, "they had decided on this big *Shootout at the OK Corral* scene where the three of us go in and beat up the bad guys. We said it was absurd and had nothing to do with the quality of the story, and they said, 'Yeah, but you can't have a movie with three Mitchums and not have a fist fight!'" Mitchum shrugs. "That's the kind of mentality we were working with."

The Mitchums went ahead with the project, figuring once the filming began they could make the story as good as possible. It didn't work out that way.

Critics savaged the movie.

"Yeah, we got murdered by the reviews," he sighs. "They compared me with my father, saying he was a better actor. Sure, he's a better actor; he's done a hundred more movies than I have."

It isn't easy to be compared constantly to someone else, in this case your father, a famous movie actor. An unfriendly press, waiting for years for a chance to lash out at the elder Mitchum for his disdain of the media, has a tendency to ask damaging questions, to take statements out of context. Chris Mitchum, as well as his older brother, Jim (who does look strikingly like his father), knows how it feels to be a media target.

"When I was going to school in Philadelphia, I'd only get to see my father a couple times a year," Mitchum says. "I'd agree to an interview and the article would come out headlined 'CHRIS MITCHUM AND FATHER ESTRANGED—ONLY SEE EACH OTHER TWICE A YEAR.' The press would try and build an 'I-hate-my-father' routine.

"It's hard because I hate talking about it. For twenty years I've been hearing the same questions, so when I feel uncomfortable, I simply say, 'I really don't want to talk about it.' He shakes his head. "Then I'm asked, 'Why *don't* you want to talk about it? What are you hiding?'"

Yet Chris Mitchum's boyhood memories of his family are happy ones. "It was a very normal childhood," he affirms. "My father always shunned the Hollywood limelight. We lived in a little house in which my parents raised the three of us—my brother Jim and younger sister Petrine. Dad went off to work, and sometimes I'd go with him and hang out at the studio.

"In the early years, when my father was making westerns with Hopalong Cassidy, I'd go down to RKO and see him on the set, but I was more interested in the miniature department and seeing the two-foot-tall King Kong or the five-foot-long aircraft carrier."

How does a child reconcile the reality of a father at home reading the newspaper to the fantasy image of a movie actor punching villains out on the screen?

Chris Mitchum smiles, remembering the first time he realized his father was a movie hero. "I knew he would go to work and stand in front of this camera, and that his picture would end up on the screen, but I had never seen him in a movie. I'd go to Saturday matinees and see a cowboy idol like Lash Larue in a western and root for him, but I never made the connection to see my father in the same way.

"Then, when I was eight years old, the family was driving cross-country, and every time we'd stop there'd be fifty people around the car getting his autograph. I kept wondering why all these people wanted him to sign papers. It all seemed so bizarre to me. When we got to Los Angeles my mom took me to a movie, one of the Hopalong Cassidy westerns. She told me I was going to see my father on the screen—and not to say anything." Mitchum settles back into the soft chair and looks up wide-eyed, as if he is seeing a movie screen. "And there he was—leaping off a building onto a horse!" Mitchum stands up, finger pointed at the imaginary screen. "'Hey Mom, look! There's Dad!' It stunned me. There's my dad on the screen—just like Lash Larue. And with Hopalong Cassidy!"

Although he had discovered his father was a movie actor, young Chris Mitchum decided he didn't want to be a performer. He wanted to be a writer and a teacher. To achieve that goal, he enrolled as a literature major at the University of Arizona. He had already married and fathered two children. Fiercely independent, he continued his studies and provided for his family by working as an extra at Old Tucson, a western village where production companies would come to film cowboy movies. "I was making $13.80 a day as an extra," he says. "In 1967 you could have a couple meals on that kind of money."

A film production manager saw the young literature student and told Mitchum that if he were ever in Los Angeles to look him up. The manager promised him an acting job. Mitchum's doctorate and the $18,000 a year he'd make as a teacher looked a long way off. So he went to Hollywood.

"I got a day's work playing a dead man in a movie," he remembers. "That was my acting debut. I didn't blow any lines." He grins at the bad joke.

Mitchum then landed a job on a production crew as a gofer—someone to "go for" cups of coffee. Later in 1969, he was working as second assistant director on a low-budget film called *Bigfoot* when the director asked him to take the lead.

"I played the long-haired, hippie leader of a motorcycle gang whose girlfriend is kidnapped by the monster. It seemed the bigfoots were dying out so they were breeding humans. The plot was a little sordid."

Then he got a two-liner part in *Chisum* starring John Wayne. "The Duke came up to me and said"—Mitchum changes his voice into a startlingly good imitation of John Wayne—"'Ya know, you shoulda played Billy the Kid.'" Mitchum shakes his head. "I didn't think he knew I was on the set."

Director Howard Hawks screen-tested Mitchum for *Rio Lobo,* and the next thing the young actor knew, he was costarring with John Wayne.

"That's when I changed my mind about being an actor," Mitchum says. "What an easy way to make a buck." The phrase sounds like an echo of his father's words; Robert Mitchum has often been quoted as saying, "Acting sure beats working."

"It was exciting starring with John Wayne, a living legend," Mitchum remembers. "When I first saw him, he seemed as big as he was on the screen, fourteen feet tall with a booming voice and tremendous presence. It was like working with someone who was the fifth face on Mount Rushmore."

After making a second film with John Wayne, *Big Jake,* Mitchum began his career as an action hero in movies made in Europe and Asia as a Kung Fu star. In 1981 he won the Golden Horse Award, the Chinese equivalent of an Oscar.

"I've come into my own," he says happily. "For a long time I saw myself loitering on the threshold of success. I finally fell though the door."

Getting through that door to acting fame was much easier for another member of the Mitchum dynasty than it was for Chris Mitchum. Carrie, his daughter—he has two younger children, Jenny and Kian—has starred on the afternoon soap opera, "The Bold and the Beautiful."

"Her story is incredible," Mitchum says. "She started off as a business management major in college, then went to UCSB after we moved to Santa Barbara and enrolled in the drama department. She told me, 'Dad, I love acting. I want to go to the Neighborhood Playhouse acting school in New York.' After a year she came back to Los Angeles, took a job as a waitress, and was offered a movie role with explicit nudity, which she refused. Then she was chosen to be on the soap. The first year on the show she grossed $150,000, which isn't bad for an actress right out of acting school!"

Mitchum shifts around in the sofa chair. "She came home for a visit after her first few weeks on the soap, and as she was leaving—it was so sweet—she turned to me and said, 'Dad, if you need anything . . . money . . .' She's really happy with what she's doing."

Mitchum has begun to think about returning to his first career—writing.

"I started out wanting to be a writer," he says. "I wrote a script called *Soldiers of Fortune*. It's to *Rambo* what *Butch Cassidy and the Sundance Kid* was to westerns, a movie about relationships and humor rather than blowing everybody's guts out. I'd also like to produce, perhaps direct—a full creative process."

He stands up and stretches his lanky frame in the light from the window. "What I really wanted to be when I was growing up was a cowboy." He pauses. "I guess what I want to be is the next American western star."

Sure, why not? One can easily imagine a western starring Chris Mitchum as the white-hatted hero, his son Bentley as the hotshot young gunfighter, and his daughter Carrie, bold and beautiful as the enduring pioneer woman. And then there's the tough old rancher . . .

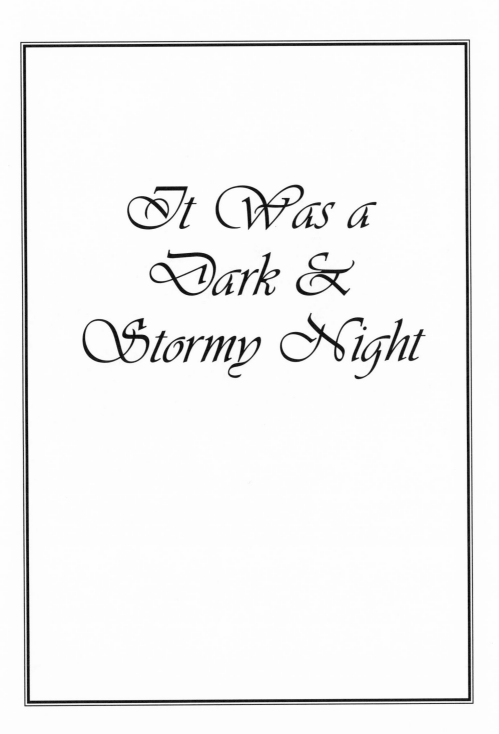

It Was a
Dark &
Stormy Night

Barnaby Conrad

Charles Schulz
Working for Peanuts

"It was a dark and stormy night . . . "

OVER forty years . . . fifteen thousand comic strips . . . drawn by one man . . . without any help?

Good grief!

"People say to me, 'I suppose you don't draw your strip anymore, do you? I suppose you're at an age where you can take it easy.'" Charles Schulz, creator of the *Peanuts* gang, shakes his head incredulously, and his softly modulated voice rises. "I still draw that strip every day!" He pauses, then adds. "Nobody else is going to draw that strip. Nobody is *ever* going to touch a pen to the thing."

You mean—*gulp!*—when Charles Schulz goes, Charlie Brown goes with him? Aren't comic strips supposed to go on forever? Look at *Gasoline Alley, Blondie, Mary Worth* . . .

"I thought about this several ways," Schulz continues. "In the first place, what difference does it make to me? I'll be gone. Then I thought, what if the family needs the money? Why should I be temperamental

147

and deprive them of an income because of my own selfishness?" (Not likely for a cartoonist who has placed fourth on *Forbes* magazine's list of the entertainment world's top money-makers. Schulz's present estimated two-year gross: $55 million.)

"My kids agree with me," Schulz continues, "They told me they didn't want anyone else to draw Dad's strip. They like what I draw and don't want anyone to spoil it like so many comic strips have been spoiled. We had it put in a legal contract: When I go, the strip goes with me."

Charles Schulz smooths a wisp of gray-blond hair from his forehead and moves his patio chair further under the table umbrella. Triangles of light, reflections from the nearby pool flicker across his face, mirroring themselves in the brown-rimmed glasses. The cartoonist is sitting poolside at the Miramar Hotel in Santa Barbara, having just finished an hour's talk for the 300 writers attending the Santa Barbara Writers Conference. He loves to meet writers, enjoys their ideas, words and books, and tries to attend the conference every year.

Schulz looks tanned and fit and relaxed—but he doesn't look like a cartoonist. What he looks like is a kindly corner druggist. He is rich and famous, shy and anonymous, a walking American Express commercial. He is not a funny man in person, nor does he get visibly angry. The strongest oath one can hear from his lips is, "Good grief!" What Charles Schulz does better than anyone else in the world of comic strips is make funny a drawing of two children standing behind a wall, talking. And he would like to be able to do that forever.

Several years ago he had bypass surgery and later hurt his knee skating (ice hockey is his favorite sport) and had to have surgery for that. "My drawing hand is a little shaky," he admits, then adds, "That's because I'm old!" (He was born in 1922.)

Schulz becomes pensive. He's been thinking a lot lately, he says, about himself, about his comic strip, about his alter ego, Charlie Brown.

"I still do some good work. I just finished a batch of strips that are pretty good." He relaxes back in the metal chair. "It's not often that you draw things you are really proud of. I've always wanted to draw something that was as good as what Charlie Chaplin did on film, or one that could make people laugh like Laurel and Hardy did."

Behind his glasses, his eyes glaze over as the images of past comic strips form in his mind, *clicking* from panel to panel . . .

CLICK.

Charlie Brown says to his fuss-budget friend, Lucy, "Do you ever wonder if God is pleased with you?" Lucy answers, "He just has to be."

CLICK.

Charlie Brown is sitting on a couch with his uninhibited little sister, Sally. He's reading about David and Goliath, and mentions that the fight ended when David hit Goliath with a stone. Sally says, "I wonder what Goliath's mother thought about that?"

CLICK.

Charlie Brown opens his mailbox on Valentine's Day and asks, "Any valentines in there?" Mouth awry, he sighs, "Nothing echoes like an empty mailbox."

Then the images are gone. At least until the next day's funny papers. And the next day's . . . and *Good grief!* A comic strip every day, 365 days a year . . . How does he keep on doing it?

"Filling those four squares is like having a term paper to do every day," Schulz admits. "If it's a good day, I can draw four strips. Drawing three is a satisfactory day, but if I only draw two it's not a very good day. Drawing six strips has only happened maybe ten times in all those years; they would have to be simple strips with Snoopy who is easy to draw."

Schulz likes to say that a cartoonist is someone who draws the same thing day after day without repeating himself. "People want to see Dagwood run into the mailman," he says, "or see him make those gigantic sandwiches. They don't want to see the same gag, but they want to see variations on themes."

Schulz glances at two children as they jump into the pool and splash furiously at each other. One has to wonder—does the cartoonist get his ideas from observing kids? Does he sneak around playgrounds, sketch pad in hand?

"I never hang around playgrounds," he says, smiling. "I'm always asked if I get a lot of ideas from my children." (He has five children by his first wife. They were divorced in 1972 after twenty-one years of marriage. Two years later he married Jeannie Forsyth, an energetic woman who has a passing resemblance to actress Jane Wyatt.) "One day the family counted up the ideas they had given me in the last forty years and decided it was sixteen.

"My daughter, Jill, came up to me one day when she was quite small and told me she had just discovered something. She said: 'If you hold your hands upside down you get the opposite of what you pray for.'"

CLICK.

"Jill and her sister, Amy, were making real nuisances of themselves one evening at the dinner table, and I said, 'Can't you quiet down? Do you have to chatter all the time?' Amy didn't say anything; she took a piece of bread and started smearing it with butter. Pretty soon she looked at me and pouted, 'Am I buttering too loud for you?'"

CLICK.

Schulz, who planned on going to art school on the GI Bill after World War II (he was in the army), says he "rarely sketches for fun," but feels he can draw "pretty well." He adds, "I can probably draw better than the comic strip indicates."

Good point. It looks easy. Anyone could learn to draw those little kids—and that silly dog.

Schulz grins. "That's the secret, to make it *look* easy. But it is very difficult to know what to put in and what not to put in. I think I've always been good at expression. You know, as soon as you look at Charlie Brown, or Linus, or Snoopy, you know exactly what's happening.

"Snoopy is my favorite character to draw because he's the easiest. You draw the top of Snoopy's head, and the nose starts to appear and then you've got the whole thing. With Charlie Brown's head it's either there or it isn't. He's the hardest.

"Linus is fun to draw. I like to draw wild expressions on him; like

150

when Lucy is yelling at him. I'm very proud of the overall character of Linus. I think he's the most well-rounded individual of the group.

"Peppermint Patty is also fun to draw because she's so flexible. I love doing wild things with her hair: She falls asleep in school then suddenly says, 'I'm awake!' and she leaps up and her hair flies all over. That's when drawing is fun. That's when you're doing real cartooning."

Schulz "cartoons" each day, walking from his home at Number One Snoopy Place to his studio, then lunches with some of his cronies at the Redwood Empire Arena, a skating rink he had built in his small California town just outside of San Francisco. He rarely travels, preferring a quiet life in the company of a few friends—and his comic strip kids.

Peanuts, as we all know, is composed entirely of children, plus a dog—a huge-nosed beagle without a single redeeming virtue save being funny—and a bird called Woodstock. Adult characters are always off stage.

"When I first began to draw cartoons," Schulz says, "I discovered adults weren't needed. If you draw a strip where a crazy dog is sitting on the dog house writing novels or chasing the Red Baron in a bullet-riddled doghouse, there is no room for adults. An adult would destroy the whole fantasy, which the kids accept."

One of the unique aspects of Schulz's comic strip is that the panels are drawn from a child's viewpoint, a grass-level perspective. Schulz admits he never went in for a lot of fancy "camera angles," like Hank Ketchum. "When he draws *Dennis the Menace* he does some wonderful light and shadow angles. That's great, but it doesn't work for my type of humor." He smiles. "I've always said I'm the only one who draws grass from a side view."

Ideas and drawing are two of the elements that have made *Peanuts* a worldwide success. The third is a good cast of characters. Schulz says he has about twelve characters he can play around with. He sprinkles them into his comic strip, fitting them like "actresses and actors" into the scene.

"I think a character should come from an idea that has occurred to you rather than cold-bloodedly saying it's time for a new character. I can't say, I think I'll draw someone who's fascinated with fire engines. Of course, I lose some characters. I had a black character named Franklin, but I don't do racial humor so I only put him in now and then. I also rarely use Pig Pen."

Where did Schulz's "actresses and actors" come from? How were Charlie Brown, Linus, Sally and Lucy and Snoopy and Woodstock born? Charlie Brown made his first public appearance in 1947 in a cartoon feature called *Li'l Folks,* which was published in a St. Paul, Minnesota newspaper. In one of the first cartoons a round-headed kid has his arm around a dog (who looks a lot like a puppy-version of Snoopy) and is saying to another kid, "My buddy and I like to think of ourselves as being successful products of this new postwar world."

The cartoons were signed by "Sparky," a nickname Schulz had been given at birth. "In 1922, the same year I was born, a horse named Sparkplug was a big hit in the comic strip *Barney Google.* I became Sparky. I can't remember my parents ever calling me Charles."

Sparky Schulz loved the funny papers and read every comic he could get his hands on. "I used to copy *Mickey Mouse* and *Popeye* and the *Three Little Pigs,*" he says. In the mid-1940s he started drawing some kiddie cartoons and took them to a Minneapolis paper. "The editor kinda liked them," Schulz remembers, "and said he'd run them 'off and on' in the summer." The editor finally agreed to run *Li'l Folks* every Sunday and pay the cartoonist $10 per week. Schulz drew the cartoon for two years.

In October 1950, the characters from *Li'l Folks* became the characters in the United Features Syndicate's comic strip *Peanuts.*

"*Peanuts* is a terrible title," Schulz sighs, leaning his arms on the metal surface of the patio table. "Someone in the syndicate's production department, who had never seen any of my drawings, wrote down ten titles he thought would be good for a kid's strip—and *Peanuts* was one of them. Since that time, I've felt that the title should just be *Charlie Brown.*"

There were only five characters in the original strip, and Charlie

Brown quickly became the star. In one of the first strips Charlie Brown is walking down the street when a kid sitting on a curb sees him coming and remarks to another kid, "Well, here comes ol' Charlie Brown." Charlie Brown passes by. "Good ol' Charlie Brown . . . Yes, sir! Good ol' Charlie Brown . . ." The kid pauses and in the last panel adds, "How I hate him!" (Schulz now says he doesn't like that first strip because of the word "hate." "I'll never use that word again.")

After a few years, Charlie Brown began to look a bit older, more like he does today. And slowly, new characters began to emerge: Schroeder, the concert pianist; Lucy Van Pelt, the boisterous and crabby neighbor kid, and her baby brother, the erudite Linus.

Then came the Walter Mitty beagle, Snoopy.

Snoopy was first seen in *Li'l Folks* although he didn't act as mature or appear as human as he does today. Schulz feels Snoopy represents the dreams of a lot of people, the dream to win a tennis club championship, to be a novelist, or a world-famous flying ace.

CLICK.

Linus is talking to Snoopy: "Does it bother you that the Bible doesn't speak highly of dogs?" Snoopy says to himself, "Sure it bothers me, but I just turn the other muzzle."

But most of all there is Charlie Brown, who, with all his failures, is a likable kid. Charlie Brown, who can't fly a kite, kick a football, or pitch a no-hitter. Why is this loser so lovable? Schulz feels it's because his fans identify with his doubts, his anxieties. Charlie Brown's daily struggles often reflect the reader's daily struggles. Charlie Brown may fail, but he never gives up, he never stops trying. Never.

CLICK.

Charlie Brown is talking to Linus: "Let's just say that life has me beaten . . . So I give up! I admit that there is no way I can win." Linus looks at him and asks: "What is it you want, Charlie Brown?" And Charlie Brown answers: "How about one out of three?"

Yep, Charlie Brown, you're a good man. One has to wonder—is Charles Schulz like his creation?

Schulz pauses before answering the question. "Not completely, no. Because I've won a few more things than he has: I once pitched a no-hit, no-run ballgame, a game that Charlie Brown is never going to pitch." He shrugs. "I've never won much of anything since. Charlie Brown is just a caricature of all those losses many of us suffer day after day." (Charlie Brown did hit a home run in July 1993 off a girl pitcher, Roy Hobbs' great-granddaughter. Some trivia buffs may remember that Robert Redford played Roy Hobbs in the baseball movie *The Natural*.)

The late afternoon sun has edged a curved shadow across the patio table as Charles Schulz finishes the last answer. But there is one more question: How would Schulz, the cartoonist, like to be remembered?

He thinks about that for a moment. "Remembered? As somebody who drew a real good comic strip. I've done the best I could with what talent I have. I haven't hurt anybody. Peanuts has never been offensive. And I think I've broken some new ground in comic strips. He smiles, that pleasant corner druggist's smile. "That's enough, I guess."

Perhaps a thousand years from now an archeologist will uncover a fragment of a yellowed comic strip, and upon translating the few words remaining, will read this phrase:

Good grief, Charlie Brown . . .

It will be enough.

A Comic Strip Masterpiece

Charles Schulz has a favorite comic strip of his own, a Sunday panel that is, no doubt, the Charlie Chaplin act, or the Laurel and Hardy laugh, that he has searched for over forty years.

In the strip, Charlie Brown, Lucy, and Linus are on a little hill and they are looking at the clouds as Lucy says, "Aren't the clouds beautiful? They look like big balls of cotton . . ." The three of them stretch out on the hillside as Lucy continues, "I could just lie here all day and watch them drift by. If you use your imagination, you can see lots of things in cloud formations . . . What do you think you see, Linus?"

Linus point to the sky. "Well, those clouds up there look like the map of British Honduras on the Caribbean . . . and that cloud up there looks a little like the profile of Thomas Eakins, the famous painter and sculptor . . . and that group of clouds over there gives me the impression of the stoning of Stephen . . . I can see the Apostle Paul standing to one side . . ."

Lucy says, "Uh, huh . . . that's very good . . . and what do you see in the clouds, Charlie Brown?"

Charlie Brown hesitates, then says, "Well, I was going to say I saw a ducky and horsie, but I changed my mind."

Peanuts Trivia Quiz

1. *Was Charlie Brown a real person?*
   Yes. The real Charlie Brown was a good friend of the cartoonist's when Schulz was working for Art Instruction Schools, years before *Peanuts* was born.
2. *How old is Charlie Brown?*
   On April 13, 1971, Charlie Brown was eight years old. On that day Charlie Brown said in the comic strip that he would be twenty-one in 1983.
3. *Was there a real little red-haired girl like the one Charlie Brown is infatuated with?*
   Yes. Donna Johnson, a red-haired girl like the one Schulz knew and loved when he was in his twenties.
4. *What does Charlie Brown's father do for a living?*
   He's a barber, the same as the cartoonist's father.
5. *There were five characters when the comic strip originated. Who are the only two characters left?*
   Charlie and Snoopy. The other three—Shermy, Violet, and Patty—have been dropped.
6. *What are the names of Snoopy's dog relatives?*
   Snoopy has quite a family: his brother, Spike, and another (ugly) brother, Olaf; his sister, Belle, and her teenage son; plus the smart brother, Marbles, who wears jogging shoes.
7. *What character always calls Charlie Brown "Chuck"?*
   Peppermint Patty.
8. *What is Peppermint Patty's teacher's name?*
   Miss Tenure.
9. *Is Woodstock a boy or a girl bird?*
   A boy. Just ask Schulz.

10. *Where did "It was a dark and stormy night" originate?*
Schulz doesn't know: He just likes the sound of it. (The
phrase originated with author Edward Bulwer-Lytton as
the first phrase in his novel, *Paul Clifford,* published in
1830. The author was better known for his book, *The
Last Days of Pompeii.)*

Cathy Guisewite
Cathy!

"When the comic strip first began, I was horrified with the idea of calling it 'Cathy.' Not only did the character resemble me a little physically, but what I was writing about was quite personal. I didn't want friends calling me the next day, saying, 'Idiot, why did you say that about yourself?'"

S HE looks something like the Cathy of the comic strip—Lady Godiva-like hair, eyes like big black diamonds—except *this* Cathy, at age forty-three, is a svelte one hundred and five pounds and casts a chic glow in a designer dress. The cartoon Cathy looks like a Hostess Twinkie.

"I lost forty pounds," Cathy Guisewite says, standing next to the drawing board in her Los Angeles studio where comic-strip Cathy's life is sketched out on a daily basis. Scattered across the board is a flurry of half-completed cartoons, an explosion of creative clutter that overflows into a basket filled with rejected funny faces.

"It took me six years to lose that weight," she says, doing a half-turn, letting the pleated beige skirt swirl around her legs. A ray of sun filtering though the tropical trees outside the studio window brushes across her auburn hair.

"I have an obsession with food—something anyone who's eaten a

159

hot-fudge sundae while hiding in the closet will understand. I let my obsession rub off on Cathy."

Cathy Guisewite's "obsessions" have also rubbed off on a delighted readership who follow the comic strip in more than 1,200 newspapers. In the strip, Cathy—who sighs that she can "gain four pounds on breath mints"—has a chauvinistic boyfriend, Irving; a feminist, but married, girlfriend, Andrea; and a mother with a lifetime subscription to *Bride's* magazine.

Each of these two-dimensional characters, including Cathy—most of all Cathy—emanate like magic from the mind of Cathy's life-size look-alike. It must be a unique companionship, walking side by side though life with a cardboard cutout of yourself.

"When the comic strip first began, I was horrified with the idea of calling it *Cathy,*" the real Cathy says. "Not only did the character resemble me a little physically, but what I was writing about was quite personal. I didn't want friends calling me the next day, saying, 'Idiot, why did you say that about yourself?'

"So I bought a baby book, *Naming Your Baby,* and I looked through the names, but nothing suited her. She had to be 'Cathy.' To be, well, *me.*" Cathy tucks one leg under her, a position she assumes when she draws. "She's so close to how I think. Using the same name can be a little embarrassing at times, and I sometimes wish I hadn't named her Cathy, but it helps keep her true to life."

Cathy is true to life—one reason the critics and fans alike have hailed the comic strip. "People have said nice, beautiful, broad statements about what I write," Cathy says. "But what I am really writing about is gum wrappers and why I dropped the hair dryer in the toilet on the day it was important for me to look nice at the office meeting. I don't *try* and write about the big picture and the emerging new woman. What Cathy is doing is floundering in the middle of two moral ordeals or concepts: traditionalism and feminism. She doesn't know in which direction to go. She likes what she sees in both areas, so she is walking down the middle. Because many of us are walking the same line, she makes us laugh.

"For instance, Cathy is looking at an ad for 'Creamy-Dreamy-Lipstick' and tells her feminist friend, Andrea, that she wants to get some. Andrea screams, 'That's chauvinistic capitalism at its worst. All they are selling is sex, hope, and dreams!' Cathy grins and says, 'I'll take it.'"

For the cartoon Cathy, there is always hope—that's the key to the strip. She can have four hundred and forty phone calls to answer at work and twenty-seven projects overdue, and she hasn't done the laundry in two months and the bills are stacked up and the car is out of gas and the garbage disposal is broken and yet she believes with all her heart that not only will everything be done and fixed, but she will have lost fifteen pounds by 7:30 that night.

"Cathy is slowly getting her life together," Guisewite says. "In the early days—I began the comic strip in 1976—she spent a lot of time getting dumped on. Cathy was a kind of doormat, because of the way I was at that point in *my* life. Of course, Cathy will never have it all together. She has her weaknesses; her character is built on human weaknesses."

In one of the strips, Cathy tells Andrea about a new boyfriend. "Phillip is only interested in my body," she says. Assured that Cathy is finally getting it together, Andrea replies, "Well, you won't be seeing Phillip anymore." Cathy answers nervously, "Perhaps just one more time."

Nope, Cathy will never be perfect, but her creator wouldn't want her to be. "The problem with the concept of the 'New Woman' is that she is too perfect," the cartoonist says. "The women I read about in magazines and see on television are self-confident, self-assured, dynamic business people, and they are also cheery homemakers and understanding non-sexist mothers.

"Cathy has evolved over the years," Cathy continues. "I haven't consciously changed her, but the world around me has changed, and all of that has subconsciously had an impact on her. Today I write—and I do consider myself a writer first and foremost—a lot more about trying to balance different parts of a person's life. Certain things are not going to change for Cathy: food will remain a big problem, as will her relationship with her mother. She may give more enlightened speeches before she visits her mother, but the outcome will be the same—stuffing herself with mom's date-nut bread.

"I get a lot of letters," Cathy says, sitting at her drawing board, "and the best ones say they consider Cathy a real friend. This is a unique profession when you can create something that is taken personally. I love that." Cathy sighs. "On the other side are letters that say Cathy is an emotional wimp, that she is stereotypically obsessed with fashion, diet, and boyfriends, and that she is an 'insult to intelligent women.' I take those letters seriously as they remind me to let Cathy have a victorious moment now and then."

Although Cathy's comic-strip girlfriends, Andrea, and more recently, Charlene, the office secretary, have married, the cartoonist is adamant that her creation will "definitely never" wed. "It would ruin who she is for the reader if she got married. Being single is a good trait for Cathy. There's a mystery to it." Cathy laughs, a happy giggle that warms the room. "Besides, single women of the country would murder me if Cathy got married."

And is there a walk down the aisle in the future of the real Cathy? Cathy's face takes on a "Have-a-nice-day grin" as she answers, "In the beginning of the strip, people at the syndicate were afraid I'd get married and destroy everything I'd built up. They used to check on me regularly, asking, 'You're not dating anyone, are you?' 'You're not getting serious, are you?'"

With a mysterious smile on her face (as if she is about to reveal a well-kept secret) Cathy points to a playpen next to her drawing board which is stuffed with cuddly Cathy dolls, then says, "I recently adopted a baby."

She lets that sink in for a few moments then adds, "Her name is Ivy."

Like any new mother, Cathy pulls out several photographs of her baby girl, now eleven months old. With maternal pride she enthuses, "Is that a face, or what! I was in the delivery room when she was born. I went through an attorney and ended up in a matchmaker situation with the birth mother. You see, you meet at some point in the pregnancy and mutually agree that what you are both doing is right for the baby. It's a good thing because the birth mother knows where the baby is going. I also know the mother's background, so when Ivy gets older and has a lot of questions, I can tell her how much her mother loved her, and explain that she was not capable of raising her and that the adoption was an act of love on her mother's part."

Cathy puts the pictures of her daughter away. "I had fantasies about bringing Ivy to the office every day and letting her play happily in a playpen. That was *not* a good idea. But . . . I do bring my new dog, a spaniel named Zhou. The name is French and means, 'Scram, get out of here.'"

Several years ago a new character was introduced into the strip, a maniac dog, Electra. "I wanted an extravagant name for the comic strip dog; a name that had cosmic energy," Cathy says. "Electra sounded like the right name. The real reason I wanted a dog is that I felt Cathy should experience motherhood in some form. Electra has given her that, a dog that Cathy can mother and tell her frustrations to."

Fleshing out her personal frustrations was the genesis of the comic strip. "I was working as a writer in an advertising agency," Cathy says. "I was doing quite well, but I was confused about my business success and my lack of success in my personal relationships. I kept having one pathetic relationship after another.

"My mother had always taught me that the real strength of a person is her ability to move through a crisis—that every big crisis has a purpose and every little disappointment has a bright and wonderful side. So instead of wallowing in my own misery, I'd write my troubles in my diary, looking for the bright side. I got to the point where I was writing down the same tragic details over and over, and it was getting boring. So I scratched out a picture of myself eating everything in the kitchen while waiting for the phone to ring.

"I spent a lot of evenings drawing out my frustrations, and then I'd send the sketches home. They were simply a release. I didn't think I was creating a comic strip."

But Cathy's mother did. She told her daughter that many women had the same frustrations and that she should try to get her drawings published. Cathy ignored her.

Finally her mother went to the library and researched comic strip publishing syndicates, then sent her daughter a list of companies. Cathy still ignored her. That's when Cathy's mother threatened to mail the drawings herself, with a cover letter from "Mom." Cathy quickly sent her cartoons to Universal Press Syndicate, the first name on the list. A few weeks later, she got a letter back from Universal. In the letter was a contract.

"I was in shock," Cathy says, the wonder still in her eyes. "I've come to realize how amazing that day really was. I have talked to other cartoonists who have literally spent half their lives trying to get a syndicate to respond to their ideas and accept their comic strip for publication. Yes, it was a remarkable day."

Remarkable, indeed. Cathy had absolutely no art training. The sketches she had sent in were rough, almost stick-figure characters. In that first letter, Universal advised her, "Work on your art a little."

"I ran out the door and bought several books on how to draw cartoon characters," Cathy says. "I took them home and studied and practiced. I felt that I already had a natural knack for showing emotion and character in my drawings. If a comic figure felt sheepish or wishy-washy, the lines I drew would be wiggly; if the person was mad, the lines would be straight and hard. If a character was happy, the lines became soft and pleasant. If you try to 'feel' what you're drawing, it will work its way out to your hand."

Still, despite all her success and natural talent, the real Cathy wakes up each morning with the fear she has written her last good line. "Panic is part of a cartoonist's life, though an idea always comes. Sometimes, I have to force it a bit. For example, I'll go shopping for pantyhose and say to the clerk, 'I don't understand these new pantyhose.' The clerk will say, 'These are the latest thing. You've got your panty and hose all in one. It makes you look like you're not wearing underwear.' Then I think of Cathy saying, 'Why would I want to look like I'm not wearing underwear?' And all I have to do is put that into four frames.

"I do try and stay up on the latest fashions for Cathy. When the seasons change, I go out and buy all the new fashion magazines. Then I go to the mall and try things on and imagine Cathy having the experience, such as squeezing into a leopard print Spandex legging. The clothes might fit *me* physically, but mentally Cathy and I have the exact same problem."

When the real Cathy is told that today she looks like a walking fashion image, she grimaces and plucks at the rich material of her blouse and responds, "Yeah, *image*."

Looking around the studio, she adds, "When I got this place, I made a rule for myself that I would never wear blue jeans. My goal was to get some sense that the office was different from home. That's because I worked at home for thirteen years and never got out of jeans and a sweater." She spreads her arms. "This is my home away from home."

Cathy is fanatical about doing all the drawings on the strip herself. She works on the comic strip three days a week, then spends the rest of the time developing ideas for a profusion of Cathy-related products. She employs a cadre of young people, mostly women, to handle the licensing of her Cathy empire. Racks of Cathy greeting cards (Hallmark recently signed a contract to handle them) line the entry hallway, and shelves in several rooms display Cathy dolls, coffee cups, plaques, and other licensing items. Two years earlier she took control of all the Cathy products from her syndicate because—as she says—"I wanted to have more involvement in the grand plan. I felt that there was more that could be done. It was a hard choice because I had to get my copyright back from the syndicate, and ended up in a two-year legal battle."

Panic, joy, depression, satisfaction, hard work—it's all part of the cartoonist's daily routine. "I think this is the opportunity that writers dream about—to write from life. That's the richest material." She reflects, then adds, "One of my greatest pleasures is having someone send me a letter saying, 'Cathy, you said it just right!'"

She runs her fingers though her hair letting it fall in soft waves across her shoulders. "Drawing a comic strip is a humbling job because it's over five minutes after people read the morning paper. It's garbage. You have to start all over the next day. Yet, it's a gracious job as it gives you a new chance every day. I know that Charles Schulz, who has drawn *Peanuts* for over forty years, still approaches his drawing board with the same enthusiasm, the same paranoia, the same emotional angst, the same drive to get to the top, that he did when he began. That's inspiring. You see, I really *love* what I am doing."

And what does Cathy Guisewite ultimately want to achieve?

"My goal is to get through this afternoon with some shred of dignity."

And the real Cathy smiles, big.

Jackie Collins
Hollywood's Literary Lioness

"I woke up last night and thought: 'I must call
somebody in my next novel Casablanca.' It's such a
great name. I don't want to call anybody Fred or Jane
or Susan, so when three people get into bed together,
you don't know who they are."

A LITTLE over twenty years ago a very pretty young English
writer named Jackie Collins shattered the Charlotte Brontë–
Jane Austen "English woman writer" image with the publication of her
first novel, *The World is Full of Married Men.* The book was pure scandal. "Filthiest book ever printed," cried a chorus of critics. Published to
such scathing reviews, it promptly became England's No. 1 bestseller.

"*Married Men* didn't have one four-letter word in it," Jackie Collins
said years after the book's publication. "But it was one of the first books
where a woman did what she wanted to do. It was just about a man
who was unfaithful and the woman who turned the tables on him. At
the time that was a shocking thought to the English."

After that first book appeared, Jackie Collins moved to California
and went on to shock Americans with such bestsellers as *Hollywood
Wives, Hollywood Husbands, Rock Star,* and the 1993 release *American
Star.* Each new book showcased her impressive knowledge of the enter-

tainment world's sexual landscape and secured her reputation as "Hollywood's Literary Lioness."

Reviewers have referred to her works as tales of "maxi-sex and mini-morals," calling her an "expert in passion, pulp, and the pleasures of publishing profits." Collins responds with defiant good humor, saying that she feels she is "painting an accurate picture of Hollywood today."

Hollywood inhabitants have long played a game of guessing who the fictional characters in Collins's books really are. When *Hollywood Husbands* came out in 1986 everyone was asking: Is blonde-maned Whitney Cable Valentine modeled on Farrah Fawcett? Does Jack Python, the boudoir-jumping gigolo, bear more than a passing resemblance to Warren Beatty? And doesn't . . . no, she would never portray Frank Sinatra as . . . or would she? The only way to find out would be to question the author herself.

Barnaby Conrad, director of the annual Santa Barbara Writers Conference, asked Jackie Collins to break free from her daily writing regimen and give a talk to the conference's three hundred writers. Collins demurred, saying she hated to speak in front of groups. "No matter what I say, they will be disappointed," she said. Conrad countered by proposing a question-and-answer interview session. Collins happily agreed.

I met with author Jackie Collins in the lobby of the Santa Barbara Miramar Hotel thirty minutes before the scheduled interview was to be held. Collins in person is pure PR, a sizzling, made-for-Hollywood personality: Her eyes are deep, dark, and alluring; her hair—a flowing mane of auburn—tumbles over the square shoulders of her this-is-what-I-look-like-in-public costume, a figure-camouflaging jacket that flares over her hips. Her smile is genuine and she laughs heartily, a deep rumbling sound.

Collins and I sat on a flowered wicker sofa and I asked if there were any questions she preferred not to answer. She laughed, "Please don't ask me anything about my sister Joan Collins!" With that thought in mind, we walked to the conference room.

After introducing the flamboyant star author to the room full of embryonic, wide-eyed writers, Collins and I perched on high stools and began the interview.

CORK: Do you pattern your characters after real movie stars?

COLLINS: No, I never write about real people. (The audience of writers groaned in unison.) No, I really don't. Sure, I want readers to have fun guessing, so there may be a little bit of Farrah and a little bit of other blonde actresses in a character. My characters are composites. There is a reason for this: If I tried to write a fiction character based on Frank Sinatra, a real, publicized life, the reader would know what's going to happen next. That's boring. I try not to bore my readers.

CORK: The Hollywood crowd have remarked that you use them as role models.

COLLINS: After *Hollywood Husbands* was released, one woman came up to me at a party and screamed, "You've written about my husband! It's him, I know it's him!" The character she was referring to was an aging movie star who always chased women. I told her to look around the room. There were ten aging movie stars there who were known for chasing women.

Kirk Douglas came up to me at lunch one day when I was seated with several other women and said, "Hey, Jackie, I hear your new book has this great Hollywood husband in it. Who is he?" All the women at the table said, "It's you, Kirk!" He laughed and went away with that wonderful grin on his face.

Look, I'm fascinated with writing about famous men. They have all these problems that ordinary men don't have. Ordinary men complain that they don't have enough women, and famous men complain that they have too many. I was sitting in a restaurant in London last year at a table near a big glass window. Seated with me were Sean Connery, Roger Moore, and Michael Caine. Women who walked past actually stopped and pressed their noses against the glass to look. Total strangers would slip messages in their pockets. Women literally threw themselves at these men. That's why I find them interesting subjects to write about.

CORK: Where in Hollywood do you find your stories?

COLLINS: I have been fortunate to be invited to such parties as Swifty Lazar's annual Oscar bash. There, in one room, you can see everyone from Walter Matthau to Shirley MacLaine to Kathleen Turner. You name it, they're all there. I wander around and eavesdrop at tables. I call it research. I'll sit next to a couple of famous movie stars and I'll think, why are these people confiding in me? It's quite amazing and I'm very flattered by it.

CORK: What is your inspiration for deciding upon the names of your characters?

COLLINS: I woke up last night and thought: 'I must call somebody in my next novel Casablanca.' It's such a great name. I don't want to call anybody Fred or Jane or Susan, so when three people get into bed together, you don't know who they are.

CORK: You say you don't cast the characters in your novels from real people. Yet, you have a say about who plays the characters once the book is filmed.

COLLINS: I get a lot of letters from people who read my books and they have visual images of what the characters look like and who they want to see portraying them on the screen. In *Hollywood Wives* the producers cast movie stars that were not right for the roles. In the future I'm going to have more control over the casting. It's more fun.

CORK: You have been quoted as saying you start a novel with a character and a title and follow the trail from there.

COLLINS: I don't plot my novels in advance and I don't know who my characters are going to be until they show up on the page. I love my characters, I actually fall in love with them. I love putting them together and watching them interact.

CORK: Is that why you use so many of them in a book?

COLLINS: I know I have a lot of characters but I just can't help it. I'll be sitting at my desk, with no one around, and these characters just come by and talk to me.

CORK: In four-letter words?

COLLINS: I write about a lot of raunchy people. Look, a writer can't sit down and say: My God, my maiden Aunt Ethel is going to read this book. You have to be free when you write in your characters' voices to let them say and do what they want to do. What amazes me is the critics who say, "Oh, Jackie Collins writes nothing but sex, sex, sex, there's sex on every page." I've searched but I can't find it. If you want sex, just look around at America's bookstores today. Check out Madonna's big picture book on sex.

CORK: Since this is a gathering of writers, let's shift our focus to the process of writing itself. How do you get your writing genes going each day?

COLLINS: The best way to write is to get out of bed—don't brush your teeth—and go straight to the study and start to write. That way you've started a writing rhythm that will stay with you the rest of the day. Half an hour later take a break and put on a track suit, no makeup, then sit down in my studio to write. I'm probably the only person in Beverly Hills who doesn't rush off to exercise class. Hey, they're not all there getting healthy, they're out there meeting men. I don't exercise. I know I should, but it's boring.

CORK: What made you begin writing?

COLLINS: I did well in English composition in England and at age ten showed some literary promise by composing dirty limericks. I'd invite friends to read them at six cents a page. At an early age I knew sex sold.

I led a very wild childhood in England. I waved at the resident flasher who used to stand and watch us kids play tennis in the park. I would wave and say, "Hey, cold day today, isn't it?"

My father was a theatrical agent and we used to go to the south of France all the time. I'd go straight to a bookstore and find Frank

Harris's *My Life* under the counter. I grew up reading Harris, Mickey Spillane, and Harold Robbins. They inspired me. I knew I wanted to be a writer, but I didn't want to write proper English books. I wanted to write *improper* American books. I ended up doing just that.

At age fifteen I became too wild and was expelled from school for smoking. My parents, who were in despair, said, "What can we do with her?" I had this sister who was eight years older, a movie star in Hollywood, and that seemed convenient so they put me on a plane and sent me to California. Perhaps I would become an actress like my sister Joan.

(In the early 1960s Collins did take a stab at acting, playing in a few movies, and television shows like *The Avengers* and *The Saint*. In a little over a year, Collins returned to England and at age eighteen married a London businessman and gave birth to a daughter, Tracy. The marriage lasted four years. In 1966 Collins married American businessman Oscar Lerman, had two daughters, Tiffany and Rory, and lived in Beverly Hills until Lerman's death in 1992.)

CORK: You started out to be an actress. Did that help you with your ability to write dialogue?

COLLINS: It helped me with my ability to understand men in the film industry!

CORK: What was the impulse for writing your first novel?

COLLINS: There are a lot of women in the audience so they will appreciate this story. I was at a party and a woman came up to me and said, "You know something? The world is full of married men." And I thought, that's my title! There are all these men chasing women, but there are no women chasing men. I took this double standard as my theme. Women loved it. Men were shocked. Men said it was the dirtiest book they had ever read. Yet, there wasn't a dirty word in it.

CORK: What's your favorite Jackie Collins book?

COLLINS: *Chances*. (She speaks the word with a soft English "a.") It was my first big bestseller in America. I loved that book, I loved the characters. It was the great American dream, a man rises from nothing to be one of the biggest gangsters in the country. His daughter, Lucky, was a strong woman. I love writing about strong women.

CORK: Is there a book you wished you hadn't written?

COLLINS: Perhaps. [Her face turns sour.] *The Bitch* wasn't a very good title. It sounded like a good idea at the time. It came about because I had written *The Stud,* a book about a man who thought he was using women, when, in fact, he was being used. It was made into a very successful movie starring my sister, whose character was the proto-type for Alexis Carrington Colby in *Dynasty.* As a sequel I wrote *The Bitch,* a real quick book. I like to write long books with a lot more— if you'll pardon the expression—*meat* in them.

CORK: What made you think you had talent as a writer?

COLLINS: My first novel was a real fly-by-the-seat-of-your-pants sort of thing. I really didn't know what I was doing; I just knew I wanted to tell a story. I still know nothing about technique; my grammar goes all over the place. But that's the way people speak. I call myself a street writer because I never sat down and taught myself how to do it. Once I took a page to my typist and said, "Fix the grammar on this." When she gave it back to me—ugh! I said, "Never do that again!"

CORK: Do you like to write?

COLLINS: When you're a writer and you wake up, the main thing you want to do is defrost the refrigerator. It seems so much more exciting than closing yourself up in a study for seven hours and shutting out the world. Even if you have a lousy headache or the cat just died, you have to get up and write. Even for me, who's written bestsellers, I find it incredibly difficult to shut myself away from the world and write.

CORK: Do you type?

COLLINS: I write in longhand. That's the best way to do it; you can write while sitting on an airplane. I used to write my books when I took my kids to school, in the car at stoplights. I write every day of the week and my secretary comes in once a week and puts everything on a word processor. I love word processors. I can't use them, but I think they're great. I rewrite the pages immediately, then my secretary can make the changes without retyping every page.

CORK: One hundred years from now, when literary historians analyze writing from the twentieth century, how do you think they will remember your books?

COLLINS: My books are definitely going to be remembered because I have captured a very accurate view of Hollywood. Yes, they will live one hundred years—or more.

CORK: One last question: Why, after making a fortune writing, do you keep on writing?

COLLINS: Because I love it. (She smiles, impishly this time.) Besides, when I complete a book, I always present myself with a reward.

CORK: A bottle of fine wine, perhaps?

COLLINS: Shall we say—*a Ferrari.*

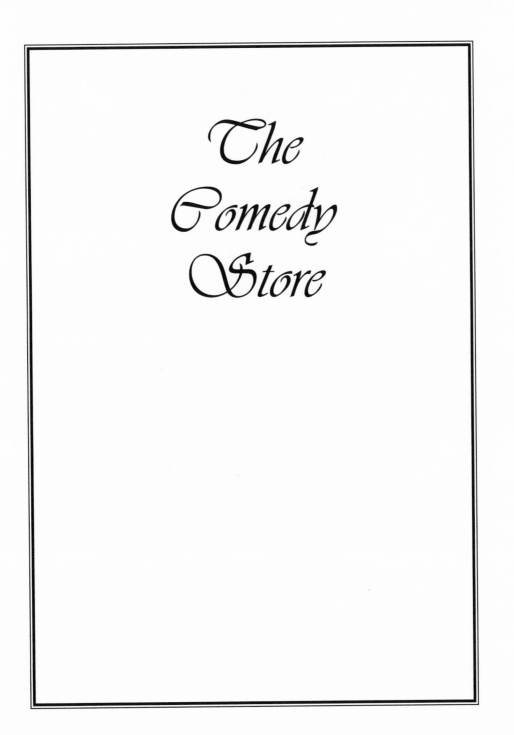

The
Comedy
Store

Barnaby Conrad

Jonathan Winters
A Season of Winters

"One publisher looked at my autobiography and asked, 'What about your affairs?' I said, 'They're in order.'"

JONATHAN WINTERS squints his face into a shriveled lemon look-alike. His mouth purses open and out comes the creaky voice of Maude Frickert, the world's oldest living airline stewardess.

"My older brother, Lamar Gene, he always wanted to fly. He kept jumpin' off roofs—broke ever' bone in his body. Then one day he stepped into the stone quarry—he'd scotch-taped one hundred and fifty-six pigeons to his arms—and he said, 'I'm gonna fly!' And with those little birds on his arms a rip-roarin', all one hundred fifty-six of them, he got off to a running start. He was airborne for ever' bit of five seconds when this kid threw a box of popcorn in his path . . . "

Jonathan Winters's face relaxes back into soft lines. "That was the longest laugh I ever got in my life. It was a funny picture—one hundred and fifty-six pigeons . . . " Winters smiles and brushes an imaginary speck from the front of the Cincinnati Reds uniform he is wearing (he has an uncanny resemblance to Babe Ruth) and adds, "I guess it was the funniest picture I ever painted."

Jonathan Winters paints thousands of funny verbal pictures, and he does it instantly. The nation's elder statesman of spaciness, and the recognized genius of comedy improvisation, he can loose lightning bolts of his own wacky brand of humor at the drop of a straight line.

"It's a matter of instantly picturing the situation in your mind and then reacting to it," Winters says. "I have to believe in my little warped mind that the audience out there will see the same picture and laugh."

Jonathan Winters is an intense man with an incredible arsenal of voices, characters, and sound effects that spring from the fertile and evidently bottomless well of his mind. He doesn't do jokes—he does people. With a knowing smirk, he says, "I always talk to my imaginary friends." He loves to transform himself into one of his fantasy friends, and for a few brief moments live the life of that character.

In 1993 Winters traveled to the Ozarks with director Marty Good and a film crew to tape a thirty-minute video called *Jonathan Gone Fishin'*.

"That one was fun," Winters says. "I played seven parts, including Maude Frickert. I put on my dress again—more popular today than ever. No script. You don't even see any fish." He chuckles at the memory, and he slouches deep into the sofa of his Santa Barbara home.

On the walls surrounding him are an accumulation of collectibles: photographs of the comedian with famous people, most of them signed, paintings (many from his own surrealistic brush), shelves of toys, walls of antique guns and knives, and autographs of entertainers from Mark Twain to Charlie Chaplin. On a hallway wall are framed letters and documents signed by every president of the United States, the more recent ones inscribed personally to Winters.

Why is Jonathan Winters obsessed with entertaining, compelled to be funny? Perhaps it's the Walter Mitty within him struggling to get out. He can't walk into a restaurant or hotel or arrive at a party without feeling the desire to transform himself into another character. One day, after lunch at the Santa Barbara Biltmore, he passed the beauty shop on the way out. Quickly stepping inside he assumed the character of a hairdresser and entertained the startled, yet delighted customers for twenty minutes.

Yet he is much more than a court jester: he is an enormously complex man with little tolerance for convention, and beneath much of his humor is the hard cutting edge of satire and strong social statement.

Like all great comedians, he is deadly serious about being funny and in sudden moments of iconoclastic fervor he will fearlessly smash any idol in his path. Mention the word *evangelist* and he is transformed into a television fire-and-brimstone preacher with a booming voice that thunders in elastic vowels across an imaginary pulpit:

"Jesus said . . . What did he say? Let me tell you—as I walk back and forth across this 275-foot marble stage—bigger than the one in Rome, I might add—Miss Kornfeld and I are not married, but we love each other. And why? Because Jesus loves her and I love Jesus and Jesus loves all three of us!"

Winters stops for a moment then adds seriously, "Those are the guys I worry about. They're reading the right book, but they're telling the wrong stuff. But then I think, well, what do I know? Charlton Heston— I prayed to him for years."

It takes very little to get Winters's impulsive mind working. A verbal challenge such as, "Jonathan, you're in Kentucky, a hillbilly sitting on a porch," and his voice quickly dissolves into a backwoods drawl and he says:

"Cast your eyes down there among those plum trees and those apple trees, fruit all over the ground, wrinkled and shriveled—my face is just like 'em. You see those cows down there? Made of tin. And those horses? Made of wood. It's just too much of a chore to go down there and feed 'em. Look at that cat, her eye is all shriveled too. Some kid poked her. But that eye will roll back before winter, just like a pinball machine. Right now the eye is white so we call the cat Little Orphan Annie."

When asked to dream up a visual image of himself Winters thinks hard for a moment, twisting and changing pictures in his mind until he says:

"I'm standing in front of a full-length mirror, nude, painting a suit on myself, putting the little white collar on, the tie . . . I'd have to shave my chest and probably my legs. I'd paint on boots, cowboy boots . . ." He laughs for a moment, liking the picture.

Images, images, images . . . pictures in his mind that reflect back to the beginning . . .

Jonathan Winters was born in Dayton on November 11, 1925. When asked what sign he was born under he replies, "Slippery When Wet." He had no brothers or sisters, which, he says, "was a great break since there was very little in the will. I got the table."

He lived with his mother, who worked in radio for thirty-five years ("kind of a watered-down Arlene Francis," Winters says), and his grandmother and stepfather. He listened closely to these older people: "I was like a gigantic sponge, absorbing everything I heard. It was like I had this fantastic movie camera on my shoulder with two lenses taking pictures and recording the sounds of people, factories, ships, and cars. All I had to do was go into the darkroom and develop what I had seen and heard."

Later he used the people he knew and had lived with in his childhood as part of his comedy routines. The grandma character, Maude Frickert, was something like his aunt Lou Perks. "My aunt was a big lady with snow-white hair," Winters remembers. "She had a great sense of humor. She wasn't exactly a dirty old lady, but maybe 'blue' old lady would describe her."

To prove his point, Winters's face turns lemon-like again and the creaky voice of Maude Frickert begins to speak:

"I'm eighty-seven years old and I've had seven husbands. But Tom, the hired boy—he's thirty—is built like a Belgian horse. He's so strong he carries me to bed every night. We play pretend, what we call 'rescue.'

He carries me up there to my room and puts me on the old quilt (Winters's eyes widen and the eyebrows go up) . . . he's a joy to have around. I just look at him all the time. He's a bronzed god. In the winter months he'll get white, but I have some stain. I keep him stained."

Winters learned by listening but he didn't listen well in school, although he says he did have a love for "art and recess." He quit school during World War II and joined the Marine Corps, where he served as a corporal stationed on the aircraft carrier *Bonhomme Richard.* "My mother said it would be just like a big summer camp," Winters recalls wryly, then sighs, "I don't have a brilliant military record, but I enjoyed the time I was in the Marines."

On the wall behind the comedian is a framed set of Marine corporal stripes, complete with a set of brass buttons, a reminder of a goal he seriously wanted to achieve. After three years of "camp" he went back to school to study art. There he met Eileen, a slim, attractive girl with sparkling blue eyes. They were married in 1948. Not long after their marriage Winters asked her why she married him. She replied, "Because you were the funniest man in my life." He still is—they have been married for over forty years.

To develop his natural ability for comedy, Winters took a job as a disc jockey at the Dayton radio station WING. Since he had no one to interview on the air he began making up characters. In the next two and a half years he developed the routines that he would use so successfully later as a stand-up comedian.

In 1953 Winters headed for New York with $56.43 stuffed in his pocket. He told Eileen that if he couldn't make it with comedy routines in a year he would return home. He made it in seven months. The Winters family, including son Jay and daughter Lucinda, lived in New York for the next eleven years.

Winters played the nightclubs and made guest appearances on Steve Allen's "Tonight Show," and the "Gary Moore Show." His fondest memory of those days is when Alistair Cook asked him to be a guest on "Omnibus." Winters was the first comedian to be asked on the show.

The comedy scene of the mid-1950s was the perfect place for Winters's satirical, nonconformist style of humor to flourish. The comedian feels the Eisenhower presidential years had begun to dull the senses and the American people were suffering from a lack of energy. Winters and his generation of comedy rebels were trying to shake people awake.

"Mort Sahl, Lenny Bruce, all of us wanted to turn this attitude around somehow," Winters says, his face now hard and serious. "We wanted them to listen. Lenny gave them a pretty good shock. He had this cattle prod that he turned on the public and, wow, they either went with it or jumped out of the way. My only criticism of Lenny—and I knew him very well—was that he wanted to get his audiences up in their seats twisting and turning, almost in agony. It worked. There were a lot of people picking up on the shock value, but I kept thinking of the families with kids and how they were worried that this stuff was getting pretty raunchy. I don't think of myself as Pat Boone, but I always argue that you can be funny without being filthy.

"You see, a comedian *says* funny things. A comic *does* funny things."

Winters gets up and walks across the living room, using it as a stage. "Laurel and Hardy were the greatest comics. No one else has replaced them: not Rowan and Martin, not Martin and Lewis—Abbot and Costello didn't even come close. Thank God once in a while someone like Laurel and Hardy comes along. They were never dirty, never told a joke, but they did funny things."

Suddenly Winters stops, changes his face and voice into that of the skinny Stan Laurel and mimics, "'What is *that*, Ollie?'"

Then Winters is the gruff, patronizing Hardy, "'That's a tarantula. Touch it and it will *bite* you.'

"'No, it won't bite me,'" the timid voice answers. "'I know a tarantula when I see one.'"

Winters scratches his head à la Stan Laurel, reaches out, then quickly pulls his hand back. "'Ouch! It *did* bite me.'

"You can make anybody funny," Winters says, back in his own voice. "There are a lot of raised eyebrows about that, but you can. You can put funny clothes on them, or you can give them funny things to do or say, but the one thing you can't do is make them *think* funny. Thinking funny, I believe, is a God-given talent."

Winters has used his talent to think funny for over fifty years, and several years ago, he decided to write some of these thoughts down on paper.

"I just sat down one day and started to write," Winters recalls. "Not with the idea of putting it on all the bookshelves of America. I thought it was time for me to write down all the things I thought were important to me. I believe I've said a lot in my comedy, but maybe I hadn't said enough. So I took my time and wrote it all down, by hand, some five hundred pages in a large artist's sketch book.

"It's a book in which I tell the truth; my feelings about doctors, lawyers, dentists—leaving you in the chair with fifty-five tools in your mouth saying, 'Sorry, Jon, I want to watch the World Series.' I talk about the toys I had as a kid, and what it might feel like to be a seagull. I try to say what I feel about laughter, sorrow and pain. I dedicated the writing to all people who are overly sensitive. They should never be ashamed of it—it beats being overly bitter. The overly sensitive are on a different frequency, and they can turn their antennas and pick up signals that are incredible. Sure, they take a lot of blows, but they live a richer life."

Winters completed the collection of vignettes that he called "short stories"—and titled them, *I Couldn't Wait for Success, So I Went On Ahead Without It.*

Random House editors looked at the manuscript, and, confused by the unfunny prose, the downright melancholy stories, asked, "What about your affairs?" Jonathan replied, "They're in order." In private, he added, "Besides, what guy runs down the roadway yelling, 'Hey, I just made it with Alma!'"

Random House decided to buy the manuscript for a $150,000 advance, mostly as a way of "starting a relationship," the publisher recalls. What Random House really wanted was a full-scale conventional autobiography, a book they expected to rack up *Iacocca*-size sales. The publisher retitled the short stories *Winters's Tales* and was astounded when it hit number four on the *New York Times* best-seller list.

Winters is now keeping a journal of his life which he has titled, *In Search of a Playground.*

"My autobiography is not a *Daddy Dearest,* or a *Mommie Dearest,*" Winters says. "But I had some unusual parents. My father said to me, 'You have to be the dumbest white boy I've ever known.' My mother was kinder to me. She just said, 'You're having the same problem I'm having. You're just slow.'"

One can still see the hostility toward his father reflected in Winters's eyes and in the tremor of his voice as he continues, "My father, who was jealous of my success, came backstage one time and said, 'I knew you were queer—you're wearing a goddamn dress!' And when I told him I got $10,000 for wearing it, he said, 'Well, I wouldn't wear it for a million dollars.'

"I just said to him, 'My mother told me you were an asshole, and she was right.'"

Winters has penned the first paragraph of his autobiography. It begins: "I was born on November 11, 1925. My mother, I'm sure she said, 'I'm sure it's a boy, hold it up again.'"

Also in the autobiography will be moments of joy that Winters will cherish forever. One of his favorite moments came when he shook the hand of astronaut Neil Armstrong. At that meeting the comedian said simply, "Dayton, Ohio," and Armstrong said, "Boy, do I know you! I'm from Wapakoneta!" And Winters thought, "My God, this man who came from a town about the size of this room—we didn't even play them in football—is the first man to step on the moon!" Meeting Neil Armstrong was doubly important to Winters because forty years earlier he shook the hand of the man who had climbed the first rung of the ladder into space, Orville Wright. Two of Winters's most cherished possessions hang side by side in gold frames on the wall: autographs of both Orville Wright and Neil Armstrong.

Looking fondly at the autographs, Winters recalls, "My grandfather, Valentine Winters, who had a great sense of humor, knew Orville Wright, and one day he asked him, 'Why did you have to go all the way to Kitty Hawk to find air!' "

Winters has always wanted something published with his byline. In 1965 he sold a little book of his drawings titled, *Mousebreath, Nonconformity and Other Social Ills.*

"It sold fifty-one copies," he says. "Mostly to small institutions. The patients threw them at each other. One guy ate my book, but that's all right. I've done the same thing. *National Geographic* on a Sunday afternoon is delicious—just stay away from the color photos of the turtle cemetery on the Galapagos Islands."

Winters smiles at the thought and sinks deeper into the couch and pats his stomach, perhaps thinking about lunch only an hour away. On the wall opposite of him is one of his paintings, a vivid splash of color and images titled *Conductor In Space.* It is a surrealistic fantasy that might be compared to the canvases of Paul Klee. Winters paints extemporaneously, the same way he breaks loose in his comedy routines. The paintings are of motion and whimsy, a happy array of colors that sparkle joyfully against one another.

"I started out to be an artist," he says. "Why did I quit? Starvation was a factor. But the truth is I didn't have a style." It took twenty-five years before the comedian discovered his own artistic style and began painting again. In 1975 his canvases were featured at the Ankrum Gallery in Los Angeles. He sold 95 percent of his paintings at that show, and received outstanding reviews from art critics.

Random House, impressed with the sales of *Winters's Tales,* released a 1988 coffee-table book of Jonathan Winters's surrealistic paintings titled *Hang-Ups.* Winters thumbs through a copy of the elegant book as he says, "I enjoy the privacy of art. It's fun to go up to my studio"—an eight-foot by eight-foot loft above a gallery of his canvases, all of which, as the inveterate collector, he is reluctant to part with—"and dabble with a brush. In painting I think it's important to see something on canvas that you can recognize. I feel there is too much in modern art that is a cop-out for people who can't draw or paint. I can't believe that you can take cobalt blue acrylic paint and throw it against a fifty-five by sixty foot canvas and say it belongs in a museum. First of all you have to learn how to draw. Learn anatomy, and if you can't—go to drawing chickens, quick."

Jonathan Winters: painter, writer, comedian—what's next? Is there some last elusive piece of the master jigsaw puzzle? The answer is yes—one last piece.

"I want desperately to perform in a good dramatic film," Winters says. "I'm not trying to prove anything, it's just something I want to do. I think I am capable of it. I've come close a couple of times. Once with a Rod Serling 'Twilight Zone.' I did the movie *The Loved One,* which was more of a comedy satire. My first big movie break was *It's A Mad, Mad, Mad, Mad World.*

"I may never do one bigger than that," he adds.

"I've seen some of my contemporaries turn the corner and go dramatic. Alec Guinness went from being a comedian on the screen to being a dramatic actor of great force. I've seen Red Buttons, Ed Wynn—God, the people—Jackie Gleason . . . my friend Robin Williams . . ."

Winters got partway to his dramatic goal when he won an acting Emmy in the 1992 comedy series *Davis Rules.* In the show, Winters played Gunny Davis, a loopy but lovable grandfather figure. The director encouraged—actually *instructed*—him to ad-lib and improvise, and offered five minutes of space for Winters's impromptu riffs. In one scene, before retiring for the night, Gunny announced, "I got the bedroom window closed, but the cat is halfway out." He gave an eye-rolling shrug. "I guess it can wait 'til morning."

Winters was so sure he wouldn't win the Emmy, he opted not to attend the 1992 award ceremonies, a decision he regrets today. "My wife decided we should have dinner with friends," he says sadly.

Winters pauses, then says seriously. "I think of myself as a survivor." He smiles quickly, not wanting to become morose, and changes to comedy. "I want to be buried in a baseball uniform with a parking meter above me. You slip a nickel or a dime in and you can talk to me through the grass. No, I think it would be better to be cremated. I see no reason to water something that isn't going to come up. I just don't want to take up any space. I have taken up a lot of space and time in my life." He stands, stretches, winds up an imaginary baseball, and throws it through the screen door. Yep, Babe Ruth.

There are a lot of Walter Mittys walking around out there, dreaming their own secret fantasies, pretending they are Superman, Bluebeard the pirate, Robin Hood—or even Babe Ruth. Winters is only one of them.

He just happens to be the funniest.

Barnaby Conrad

Steve Allen
Hi-Ho, Steverino!

"My grandson was on my lap playing with my hair
when he asked, 'Grandpa, do you know your hair
is dead?'"

IT'S a rug, of course. And this morning it's slightly askew, like it
was grabbed from a hat rack on the way out the door and plopped
on his head. His tweed sport coat hangs loosely on his frame, shoulders
slightly stooped, the collar of his green shirt unbuttoned. The eyes are
round saucers, glazed in the light from midday sun.

Steve Allen is a tired performer.

The previous evening he had driven back to Los Angeles, watched his
wife Jayne Meadows perform in a play, then hurried back to Santa
Barbara (a two-hour trip), caught a few hours sleep, and was now sitting
at a table signing copies of his recent book, *Hi-Ho, Steverino!*, a compendium of his adventures in the "Wonderful Wacky World of TV."

The line of ladies waiting for his "Best Wishes" and scribbled "Steve
Allen" inscription are gathered for the annual CALM Author's Lunch, a
charitable event (CALM is an acronym for Child Abuse Listening

Mediation) that attracts 550 guests to the ballroom of Fess Parker's Red Lion Resort in Santa Barbara.

Using an informal format, celebrity authors are interviewed in front of the attendees rather than being asked to give a lecture. It is entertaining and informative presentation—and sells a lot of books, for which CALM shares the proceeds. Such authors as Michael Crichton, Ray Bradbury, Sue Grafton, Fannie Flagg, as well as celebrities Julia Child, Jane Russell, Charles Schulz, and Jonathan Winters, have participated in the past.

On this occasion, I have been scheduled to interview Steve Allen. After a lunch of poached salmon, the interviews begin. There are three other authors and interviewers on the program, each allowed twenty minutes, and as they entertain, I note that Allen, sitting at the head table, shadows his eyes with his hands, catching a catnap.

He is startled awake when the luncheon moderator calls his name, and I lead him to the dais. Settling into armchairs, microphones in hand, I ask Allen the lead question I had prepared for Zsa Zsa Gabor the previous year, one she was not available to answer as she canceled—some said "copped out of"—her appearance:

"I understand you have mirrors on your bedroom ceiling."

Allen responds without the blink of a tired eye:

"The mirrors are reversed. I see the people upstairs. It's better than watching the midnight horror movie."

Realizing it would be prudent not to try and upstage a master, I play the straight man during the rest of the question/answer session. After all, Steve Allen is a master of almost every creative endeavor: He has written 4,000 songs, including "This Could Be the Start of Something Big," and "South Rampart Street Parade," authored thirty-eight books, created and hosted the "Tonight Show," starred in motion pictures, most notably *The Benny Goodman Story,* and was inducted into the TV Academy's Hall of Fame. Andy Williams once said, "Steve Allen does so many things, he's the only man I know who's listed in the Yellow Pages."

I continue by asking a question about one of his achievements that is little known, but one that he is proud of having accomplished.

CORK: Some years ago, the nation's jazz critics waxed ecstatic about an album by a deceased black boogie-woogie specialist named Buck Hammer. I understand the name was a pseudonym. What was the real name of the pianist?

ALLEN: I've played quite a number of practical jokes in my life, but this one might be the best. Twenty-five years ago I released a boogie-woogie album. Rather than putting my name on it, I created an imaginary deceased black gentleman named Buck Hammer, whose picture was rendered as art work on the album cover. The critics loved it. One New York critic even went so far as to say, "Mr. Hammer's death was a tragic loss." They evidently figured I had contributed more as long as I was black and dead, rather than white and alive.

CORK: How do you get the creative juices flowing?

ALLEN: Three weeks without employment will do it.

CORK: When does the creative impulse strike you?

ALLEN: I can't predict when my creativity will pop up. I used to make notes on the backs of envelopes, but then I would find those notes a week later if I wore the same jacket, and have the problem of trying to decipher them. I am very unhappy with my memory. Today, I reach in my pocket and produce this (he holds up a microcassette recorder), and talk my idea into it at once. I have never lost an idea since I began using this twenty years ago.

CORK: Where do your creative ideas originate?

ALLEN: The science of psychology has no idea where anybody's creative ideas come from. It is the profoundest of mysteries: from geniuses who compose great works of art, to those who are writing little poems or essays in school. The classic explanation for the cause of this remarkable creativity is, of course, utter nonsense. On one hand they attribute philosophical treatises to the muses, and the second is to attribute all the marvelous songs and poems to God. Yet most of

193

the artistic creations of the world are lousy. That is a simple fact. Most plays are lousy, most movies are lousy, most television shows are lousy. I really don't think we want to blame God for all that stuff. Genetics is the direction we are currently looking to find the explanation of creativity . . .

 (He drops his head on his shoulder and snores—in boredom. The audience laughs heartily.)

CORK: You have written a series of novels in which you play the detective protagonist. Somerset Maugham once said, "There are three rules for writing the novel—unfortunately, no one knows what they are." (Allen laughs, his eyes brighten.) Since this is a writer's luncheon, perhaps you could share how you go about writing.

ALLEN: In the detective books, of which I have written five, the ideas were given to me. A publisher said his company had a concept for a series of novels in which Jayne and I would be the leading characters, a little like the *Thin Man* series.

 My first two novels were very autobiographical. One was called *Not All Your Laughter, Not All Your Tears,* which some of the audience may recognize as a quotation from Kellogg's All-Bran.

CORK: (I hold up a copy of his latest book, *Hi-Ho, Steverino!*) This is your latest in the autobiographical series.

ALLEN: It is in the autobiographical context or category, but it is *not,* quote, my autobiography, because it only covers fifteen years of my life in television. I am now working on a second book which will refer to the post-TV portion of my life.

CORK: Let's go back to the 1950s and the "Tonight Show." How did you create the show?

ALLEN: I would be perfectly willing to take a deep bow for something I have done, but not for the creation of the "Tonight Show," because it wasn't an original idea. I'm serious. I figure that many years ago someone was sitting on the stump of a tree in the forest someplace and a guy walked by and said, "Hi, George, how you doing?" And the guy on the stump answered, "Pretty good. How about yourself?"

And that was the genesis of the "Tonight Show." I simply brought the idea into television.

I started doing comedy on radio, and that required writing a script before the broadcast. One night Doris Day didn't show, and I had a half hour of air time to fill. I kept checking my watch, saying, "She'll be here any moment," then ad-libbing funny lines. It was the first time in my life that I was doing on radio what I had done all my life anyway—making funny remarks. I thought, hmmm . . . I didn't know you could make a living talking. It didn't require rehearsals or preparation. That set the mode of what I did on television, and became an important part of the "Tonight Show." To be a host of a talk show doesn't require talent. (There is an "Oh, sure" groan from the audience.) I'm serious.

CORK: Your "Sunday Night" prime-time show of the late Fifties, which succeeded the "Tonight Show," is best remembered for the Man-on-the-Street routines. How did that originate?

ALLEN: I created the sketch simply as a satire of the ancient and still popular journalistic cliché called Man on the Street or Vox Populi, where a question-of-the-day is asked and the answers, along with a close-up headshot, are printed. On the television show's version there was very little ad-libbing.

Louis Nye as Gordon Hathaway, the fey advertising man, would say, "My name is Gordon Hathaway, and I'm from Manhattan. Hi-Ho, Steverino! Move over Big Ben, I'm clanging tonight!" and the audience would howl.

Don Knotts, the trembling little guy, had a routine that went this way:

Knotts: My name is B.F. Morrison. I'm from New York, and I'm a carnival knife-thrower . . . retired.

I'd say: What does the B.F. stand for?

Knotts: Butterfingers.

Are you nervous?

Knotts: Noop!

Tom Poston was the guy who could never remember his name. And Bill Dana could get a laugh by just using an accent: "My name—José Jimenez."

Zany Dayton Allen's invariable response to the weekly question became a national catchphrase (finger pointing skyward): "Whyyyyy not!"

In 1988, the nation's comedians, comedy writers, and producers honored five performers for lifetime achievement in comedy. Four of them were Jonathan Winters, Sid Caesar, Woody Allen, and Groucho Marx. The fifth was Steve Allen. I ask Steve Allen to name his favorite comedian.

ALLEN: Dan Quayle. No one had to write his material for him, only repeat what he said.

CORK: Who do you laugh at most today?

ALLEN: My nine grandchildren. My grandson was on my lap playing with my hair when he asked, "Grandpa, do you know your hair is dead?"

With that, I note that our twenty minutes are up. It was a brief look at a funny man whom the *Washington Post* described by saying: "There probably hasn't been a more durable, versatile, able, and admirable personality in the history of the medium. Allen probably has been responsible for as much laughter as anybody on television." *Newsweek* added, "Steve Allen is a comedic giant—quite simply one of the most talented people in the world."

Afterward Steve Allen signed more books. The shoulders no longer sagged, the eyes were brighter, the pen quicker—and the toupee, well, it didn't appear quite so dead.

Steve Martin
Wild and Serious Guy

"The biggest loss at being a celebrity is you can't go anywhere as an observer. You can't have fun like everyone else. You can't go to a park, a zoo, or a patio café. People are always watching you . . . lurking behind trees . . ."

STEVE MARTIN is sitting with three friends at an umbrella-shaded table in a Southern California restaurant. Even without the toy arrows through his prematurely gray hair, he is instantly recognizable. And he knows it. He sips from a cup of coffee and listens to the bubbling water of the patio fountain. Then, he feels one coming—*a Steve Martin fan*. He hunches over, pulls the collar of his jacket around his neck, and shifts his eyes warily behind the jet-black sunglasses.

A large woman in a print housedress jiggles up to him. She giggles and thrusts a napkin and a ballpoint pen in front of Martin's face. He smiles wanly and scribbles his autograph on the napkin. She blabs happily and then wobbles away across the patio flagstones. Returning to her table, she whispers to her husband, "He didn't even say anything *funny*."

That is difficult for Steve Martin. He doesn't carry around a stock of one-liners like Bob Hope or George Burns, nor can he "turn on" at the drop of a straight line like Jonathan Winters or Robin Williams. Yet because he was the most phenomenally successful comedian of the 1970s, he is expected to "say something funny." To his fans he will always be that happy "jerk" on stage, that "wild and crazy guy" with the child-like comedy, the happy feet, the rabbit ears, and the balloon animals.

Unlike his stage and screen persona, Martin is a very serious man. "Steve really is bright and sophisticated," says Shelley Duvall, who starred with him in his hit movie *Roxanne*. He is also a very private man. His personal and past relationships with Bernadette Peters are taboo, as is the time he spent with Linda Ronstadt. When his busy moviemaking schedule permits, he and his wife, Victoria Tennant, travel to their weekend retreat in Santa Barbara, a home built like a concrete bunker, more ominous than inspiring. Martin's obsession is collecting nineteenth-century art. He is a serious collector, and the walls of his home are filled with paintings by such artists as Winslow Homer and Mary Cassatt.

Other than improving his art collection, Martin wants to secure his niche as a *serious* comedy actor in motion pictures. "After I gave up the stand-up comedy routines, I really wanted to be successful in motion pictures," Martin says.

It hasn't been easy. The comedian had creative problems transferring his own wacky brand of 1970s humor to the movies of the 1980s. His first starring film, *The Jerk,* which came from Martin's fertile imagination, set him off toward his goal. It was a resounding success—with his fans, if not the critics.

Martin's next movie, *Pennies from Heaven,* an art-deco musical fantasy, confounded audiences and bombed at the box office. The comedian did little better with *Dead Men Don't Wear Plaid,* whose gimmick was to intersperse new scenes with old black-and-white footage of Humphrey Bogart and Alan Ladd. But the movie was not well-received by Martin fans.

In *The Man with Two Brains,* the jokes were zany and Martin thought he was almost on track. He and the producers were stunned when it did poorly at the box office. *The Lonely Guy* followed next and died quickly. "It was sort of a stinker," Martin admits.

Martin's search for his kind of a movie, a mix of serious comedy with burlesque bits, began to jell with the 1984 release of *All of Me* (costarring Lily Tomlin), which made use of his gifts for physical comedy. "I was very happy with *All of Me*," Martin says. "It's the first film I have done that is funny without having to think about being funny."

In 1987 came *Roxanne,* a contemporary version of *Cyrano de Bergerac.* The reviews were great. When *Time* magazine praised Martin with a complimentary cover story, he felt his movie dreams had come to fruition.

Martin's follow-up portrayal of a worried father in the disguise of a goofball in *Parenthood* has secured his place on the cinematic scene. In this rich role as the father of a modern nuclear family, he is able to balance his serious maturity with his wild and crazy instincts. At a party, Martin, in a makeshift cowboy outfit, fills in for an absent clown. The comedian is able to play a jerk—but not be one.

His movies of the early 1990s, most notably *Grand Canyon,* have made Martin a *serious* screen comedian—not just a fad like Hula-Hoops or pet rocks, not just a flash from the 1970s. He would never have to go back to being that wild and crazy guy on the stage again.

Steve Martin's comedy that came out of the 1970s was, well—weird. It was labeled silly, brainless, and Disneyesque. *Newsweek* called Martin the "ultimate West Coast wacko."

Carl Reiner once told Martin that he looked like a guy who looked at Fred Astaire and said, "Hey, I can do that—watch." The critic Pauline Kael said it more succinctly: Martin's stage act, she said, was a guy acting like a comedian and the audience acting like an audience.

"I always looked at my solo stage comedy as a success of timing," Martin says. "I had the right act at the right time. During the sixties I started formulating my comic ideas—I knew the seriousness of the social sixties would eventually pass into the silly seventies, and I was getting ready for it. When it came, I was ready. I was silly, but I was avant-garde.

"If I had to categorize myself at that time, I would say I had sort of—I wouldn't say a gift—but rather a supply of energy on stage. I was real energetic—and real dumb."

Dumb? He'd stand in front of audiences of 20,000 and turn balloons into animals or sing his one-million-selling ditty, "King Tut." He'd say: "Now, the nose-on-the-microphone routine," and he'd put his nose on the head of the microphone; then he'd say, "Thank you"—and the audience howled.

One of his comedy bits became a standard in his act, a little sanctuary, a relief, something he could thrust in when he was experimenting with a new routine and it began to fall flat. He would use it for a sure laugh: "Mind if I smoke?" he'd say, then answer in another voice, "No, mind if I fart?" It never ceased to convulse the audience.

"If I just start talking funny-type things and never give the audience a punch line, eventually their tension is going to grow so much they will start laughing on their own," Martin says. "They'll start choosing things to be funny, which is the strongest kind of humor. They have determined what is funny, not me. The laugh I like to get is 'What? I don't know why I'm laughing.'

"Beside laughs there is the real thrill of timing. That's the greatest fun of all. When you're resting, waiting, and you've got the next line in your head and you're just waiting for that little intimate moment . . . things are really flowing. Charged. Like a ballet."

How did Steve Martin, a basically shy, almost introverted "nice guy," become the goofball who paraded before thousands of people with bunny ears on his head?

"You're not going to get into my past, are you?" Martin responds when told it is time to talk about his background. "Nobody cares where I grew up. Even I don't care. When I read an interview and it gets to the part where a person grew up, I turn the page."

Martin's fascination with performing evidently began when he was ten. He was hired to sell guidebooks, Mouseketeer ears, and Davy Crockett hats at Disneyland. Then at Knott's Berry Farm, he was given the opportunity at Birdcage Theater to do his newly developed magic act and try out a few comedy routines.

From there he enrolled in philosophy at UCLA. By his senior year he had switched his major to theater arts and taken a TV-writing course. In 1968, when he was only twenty-three, he was hired to write comedy for "The Smothers Brothers Comedy Hour."

"If I wrote anything it was: 'Here's Burl Ives,'" Martin says. "It was no big deal." Writing worked for him, and at a weekly salary of $1,500, paid the bills. But he wanted to be a performer.

"Writing for TV was like learning to swallow swords," he remembers. The closest thing he got to being a performer on "Smothers Brothers" was the night he played a human head on a silver platter and spouted off several one-liners.

He was signed with the William Morris agency as a writer. "I went in and told them I was leaving television writing to be a performer," Martin says. "They said, 'Don't do it, you'll never make it.' Well, I've heard that line in a dozen movies, so I knew I could make it. Rejection is one of my accomplishments."

After "The Smothers Brothers Comedy Hour" was axed by CBS, Martin wrote for Sonny and Cher, then Glen Campbell. He still wanted to perform, and he finally began to get on the talk shows, including, of course, the "Tonight Show."

"I guess I've been on television a lot," Martin says. "Probably five-hundred times; 'The Tonight Show' thirty-five or forty times. I did a lot of crazy things on that show. One was reading a phone book to make people laugh. I'd pick up a phone book and read: 'Aaron Adams, 717 South Remington.' Of course, there wouldn't be a laugh, but I'd go on— 'Bill Black, 982 Montrose Avenue.' Still no laugh, then I'd take my arrow and put it on my head and read a sillier name, like 'Mary Ann Pinball . . .' By the time it was over, I'd end up waving a rubber chicken, and then finally say: 'Don't look at me, I didn't write this junk.'"

Martin didn't write his own material for his stand-up comedy routines. "I don't know if I could sit down and write a routine that would be funny," he says. "My original act came out of a philosophical point of view. A new point of view. I was just a guy up on a stage acting like a comedian."

Martin admits it was a marvelous feeling to play to audiences of hysterically laughing people. "Yeah, that was a thrill," he says. "But there is still the thrill of looking back and saying—'I was the biggest comedian in the world.'" He pauses, and reflects, "I will be very happy, if when I'm sixty, I can look back and say, 'I was a very funny person in this world.'"

Steve Martin has packed away the arrows through his head, he has deflated his balloon animals, and he no longer has happy feet. After all, that really wasn't Steve Martin. It wasn't even close. The real Steve Martin is a "wild and *serious* guy."

Happy
Hollandaise

Julia Child

Inside Julia's Kitchen

"I don't think I was a born chef, but I've always been hungry. At age thirty-four I could barely boil water."

"SORRY, we're having a bit of trouble with our oven," Julia Child says in a chortle that could curdle cooling bearnaise sauce. She shakes my hand, pulls me through the open front door of her Santa Barbara apartment, and propels me into the living room. "Seems rather foolish, a cook without an oven," she adds, then pops into the kitchen just as the oven man pops out.

"It's not the oven, it's the electricity," the oven man says.

"Can't you do anything about it?" Julia asks.

"You'll have to get an electrical man," he says, heading out the front door.

"What a bother." Then she turns to me, "Oh, well, nothing wrong with a cold lunch. I've got some leftover quail in the refrigerator, and some fresh asparagus, then there are always the sauces . . . come into the kitchen."

I follow this towering woman—she is six foot, two inches tall—

through a swinging door and into her domain, the kitchen. The room is surprisingly small and square with a single window over the sink. But it's a chef's paradise, with two white ovens with broilers, and a white electric stove with four burners—all inoperative. One wall is covered with copper pots, aluminum pans, wooden spoons, whisks, crushers, grinders—she calls it her "medieval torture chamber"—all the paraphernalia of a well-organized cook. A massive, thick, oak cutting table dominates the center of the room.

"I don't have room for a microwave," she says. "Besides, it takes the fun out of it. I like the sounds, sights, and smells of oven cooking." She looks disdainfully at the broken ovens as I sit on a stool next to the table.

"At my other home in Cambridge, Massachusetts, I have a bigger kitchen," Julia says as she pulls leaf lettuce from its stalk and washes the greens in tap water. "But any kitchen is fine as long as it functions as a kitchen and not something that a designer has dreamed up for *Better Homes and Gardens*. You must have the necessary cooking hardware to prepare food properly." She takes the dripping leaves and puts then into a red plastic lettuce dryer.

I watch her intently, this gastronomical giant who taught fledgling cooks—who didn't know a truffle from a toadstool—the wizardry of *haute cuisine*. Finally I ask: "What makes a good cook?"

"Good food and the love of eating," she answers pulling on the cord of the leaf dryer. The lettuce whirls inside, spinning off excess moisture. "The more 'piggy' you are, the better cook you are. Of course, having a bit of experience helps a lot. You need to know cooking terminology. It's like building blocks.

"And the more experience you have, the more interesting cooking is because you know what can happen to the food. In the beginning you can look at a chicken and it doesn't mean much, but once you have done some cooking you can see in that chicken a parade of things you will be able to create. That's when the challenge begins. That's when it becomes fun. Cooking may be a creative art, but it's also a wonderful full-time hobby."

Julia puts the lettuce in a bowl, then opens the refrigerator and takes out a small leg of smoked ham. "The problem for cookery-bookery writers like me is to understand the extent of our readers' experience. I hope I have solved that riddle in my books by simply telling everything. The experienced cook will know to skip through the verbiage, but the explanations will be there for those who still need them."

Cookbooks have been one of the key measures to Julia Child's success. The real key to the success of her books has been her ability to take the mystery out of French cooking, to move it out of the bistro and into the American homemaker's kitchen.

"My idea was to shake French cooking out of cuckoo-land and bring it down where everybody is," Julia says. "Sure, you can't turn a sow's ear into Veal Orloff, but you can do something very good with a sow's ear."

In 1989 she launched her last cookbook, a glossy volume with a $50 price tag, titled *The Way to Cook*. As large as a coffee-table book with 511 pages and some 650 color photographs, it is a (barely) portable cooking school, aimed at an audience who still eats for the fun of it. The dishes range from *choucroûte garnie* to Boston baked beans, from *boeuf bourguignonne* to hamburger.

The book also acknowledges current dietary concerns, but a bit reluctantly. Julia does not like the accusation that she is a big-time cholesterol pusher, yet has little patience with what she calls "nervous nutritional nellies."

Her tone of voice takes on an unusual fierceness as she says, "Why is everybody overreacting? People tremble at the term cholesterol. If Americans continue to have this fear of food, it will be the death of gastronomy in this country. Food is one of the simplest and nicest pleasures in life: It is there to have fun with, to enjoy."

Julia's advice is to eat sensibly but with pleasure. "You can have some olive oil, you can have some butter," she insists. "It all comes down to moderation." Julia adds that she carefully checks her weight daily, eats lots of fruit and veggies, few desserts, and generally small portions. She breakfasts with gusto on two kinds of health cereal she mixes together.

"If I didn't watch myself, I'd be a Mrs. Six-by-Six."

Yet, in the next breath she grumps, "I dislike dressingless salads and sauceless salmon and prefer carrots with loads of butter. I like marbled steaks, and I like butter. I am very careful to eat two tablespoons of saturated fat a day with greatest pleasure! I still insist an unhappy stomach is going to curdle one's nutrition."

Amazingly enough, Julia McWilliams at age thirty-four could barely boil water.

"I don't think I was a born chef, but I've always been hungry," Julia says, slicing the last of the smoked ham. "And I married a man who likes to eat. We both shared a passion for food."

The Childs have been inseparable through their long mariage—he has been her advisor, photographer, and closest friend, and he even co-autographs her books. Unfortunately, Paul Child has been in failing health for several years. "He has had several strokes and suffers the dwindles," she says.

Paul and Julia met during World War II in Ceylon (now Sri Lanka). Paul, a confirmed bachelor at age forty-two, and a career Foreign Service employee, was designing war rooms for Lord Mountbatten, and Julia was serving as a filing clerk in the Office of Strategic Services. "I joined the OSS with every intention of achieving spy status," she says.

"I wasn't going to marry anyone—until I met Paul," Julia confesses. "I guess he ruffled my nesting instincts." She laughs. "Paul was a devoted epicure and I was a mess in the kitchen. I made him brains in red-wine sauce and it all dissolved, but in 1946 he married me anyway."

Julia's cooking skills improved dramatically when Paul Child was assigned to the American Embassy in Paris.

"We got off the boat at Cherbourg and started to drive toward Paris," Julia remembers. "We stopped in Rouen and went into a French restaurant. It was there that I had my first taste of French cuisine, a sole *meunière* bubbling in parsley and Normandy butter.

"And I never got over it." Julia puts several halves of French bread into a small toaster oven which, for lack of counter space, is stored atop the refrigerator. "The food in that restaurant was so carefully prepared . . . I was amazed. I had never tasted anything like it before. I was hooked."

Once in Paris, Julia brushed up her college French with two Berlitz lessons a day. (Paul had lived in Paris in the 1920s when he learned the language and developed a love for French cuisine.) Julia enrolled in a six-month Cordon Bleu cooking course along with twelve American G.I.s. "Some of them weren't very serious about cooking," Julia remembers. "Most of them had stayed in Paris on the G.I. Bill to be near their girl friends. For those few of us who were genuinely interested in cooking, it was easy to get the chef's full attention."

Julia was fortunate to have as a teacher Master Chef Max Bugnard, then in his late seventies, who had worked with the great Escoffier. She also met Simone Beck and Louisette Bertholle, two French women who were working on a French cookbook for Americans. Julia was taken on as the team's translator, but was soon making major creative contributions to the cookbook.

The manuscript, *Mastering the Art of French Cooking,* was contracted for by Houghton Mifflin. The book was finally completed in 1958, seven years after the writer-chefs started it. The publishing company turned it down. It was too long. The three women shortened it. Still too long. They sent it to cooking enthusiast Alfred Knopf, who published it in 1961. The sales have soared ever since.

"I happened to be the right woman with the right book at the right time," Julia says. "It was the beginning of the sixties and the Kennedys were in the White House, and there was a lot of new talk about French food. Travel to Europe was also becoming easier so Americans had the opportunity to savor French cuisine."

The book's success propelled Julia into her first television show, an educational program on Boston's WGBH called "The French Chef."

"They asked me to come on a talk show and be interviewed about the book. During the show I beat some egg whites in a copper bowl to enliven the talk. The response from viewers was quite excited and I was asked to tape three half-hour shows.

"I can remember after the first taping," she continues, "I rushed home and Paul and I dug our tiny budget television out of the unused fireplace—it was so ugly, that's where we hid it—and sat down and watched this strange woman tossing French omelettes, slashing eggs about the place, brandishing knives, and panting heavily as she careened around the stove. And that's how I and educational TV lurched into our first cooking program."

Julia's success on television was not simply based on her cooking techniques or her ability to unravel the mysteries of French cooking. Her exuberance and her passion for good food were infectious. She would take short cuts, break rules, and her audience loved her for it. She would squeeze lemons through her "ever-clean dish towel," or sample sauces with her fingers. If a minor disaster happened on camera, she would scoop up the wayward item, drop it in the pan, and say to the camera, "Remember, you are all alone in the kitchen and no one can see you."

Julia opens the refrigerator, takes out a small bowl and scoops hollandaise into a sauce dish. "I'm not fazed if anything goes wrong in the kitchen. Fact is, some people accuse me of planning disasters. That's not necessary, there are too many of them that happen automatically."

As if to emphasize her point, the bell on the toaster dings, and Julia slides the French bread, a bit burned and smoking, off the aluminum tray. "See," she says looking at the crisp edges of the bread, "little disasters are easy." She scrapes the edges of the blackened toast into the sink and says, "Well, it's ready. Let's go into the dining room."

I pick up an asparagus dish and the lettuce tray and walk into the living room and to the dining table, from which a large window overlooks a balcony and the ocean beyond.

Julia puts down a plate of cold quail, then pours from a bottle of Burgundy. "Sorry it's not white wine," she says. "Seem to be out, but this will do fine. Wine is a complement to any meal."

We clink our glasses together and they ring like ceramic wind chimes. Julia says, "*Le carillon de l'amitié*. The bell of friendship."

Julia pushes a small dish toward me. "This is an interesting sauce. Try it. Goes well with the quail. It's got liver, butter, cognac and port wine in it." Then, with a spontaneous touch of merriment, she adds, "I call it a 'loose mousse.'"

When I ask for the recipe, she replies, "Actually, we don't speak of recipes anymore." She attacks the tiny quail on her dish, effortlessly separating the meat from the bone. "It's better to say 'dishes.' Recipes sound awfully dry, don't you think? Perhaps it is better to simply say, 'the food,' or 'the dish,' and that there is a recipe for it."

Between bites of salad, I wonder aloud if she ever eats junk food.

"Yes, I try everything," Julia laughs. "I'm fond of those little goldfish crackers."

"Ever order a Big Mac?"

"Yes, many times. I love a good hamburger or hot dog."

She pauses. "Airline food is inedible. I usually bring something along, even if it's peanut butter and jelly. But if you like real food, you can't eat that frozen stuff."

"Not even frozen *gourmet* dinners?" I joke.

"I don't use the word gourmet," she answers quickly, cutting a fresh green asparagus and dipping it in hollandaise. "The word doesn't mean anything anymore. 'Gourmet' makes it sound like someone is putting sherry wine in the corn-flake casserole. Someone will say to me, 'My son is going to be a gourmet cook.' And I think, what does that mean? Does he really grind raw hamburger rather than getting it out of a package? I prefer to say 'good food' and 'good cooking.'"

Dessert is a large plate of fruit and cheese: Brie, Camembert and Cheddar. I try some of each and ask, "What was your biggest cooking disaster?"

"That's one of the four or five questions everybody asks," Julia says. "What disaster? I always answer, the most recent one. Any disaster is a learning process."

"What is the second most-asked question?"

"Aren't people afraid to ask us out for dinner," she answers. "Wouldn't they be intimidated? Well, not if they know us. We're nice guests to have"—she smiles—"we're always hungry.

"Another question is what advice I give to new cooks. I answer, to be fearless. And cook! And don't try the easy thing first. Really get into something like a chocolate mousse. That will teach you how to melt chocolate and beat egg whites. Then, remember what you have done so that will go into your mental computer and stay there."

I stuff one last piece of Camembert in my mouth, dust a few crumbs of toast off my fingers, pat my stomach and thank my hostess for a lively luncheon.

On the way out of the apartment I bump into the electrician. "Hear you're having a problem with the oven," he says. "Who needs an oven?" I softly pat my overstuffed stomach again. Julia waves from the doorway and calls, *"Bon appétit!"* as I waddle away.

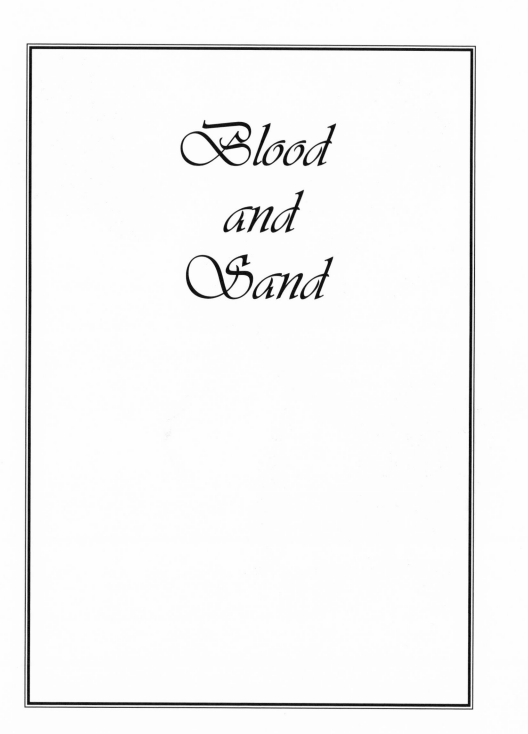

Blood and Sand

John Fulton

American Matador in Spain

"In the ring I'm aware of the sound the bull makes, the way he smells, the way it feels to have him thundering past, hooves throwing sand in front of him. I can see the sand bouncing off the hard silk of my cape and hear the rattling of the sticks, the banderillas, as the bull goes under the red muleta."

SEPTEMBER 13, 1971. On that day John Fulton, American matador, in an unusual act of defiance, jumped into a Spanish bullring with only his coat to ward off the charge of the bull—and was promptly arrested.

Today, a small piece of paper, a symbol of his frustration with mixing for forty years in what he calls the "rat race," hangs proudly framed on the wall of Fulton's Seville villa. It is the notice of a 500-peseta fine issued by the municipal police of the Spanish town of Jerez de la Frontera, a validation of Fulton's protest that he had not been given the opportunity to fight often enough in Spain. Especially that week when the Jerez Sherry Festival was being dedicated to the United States.

"You see, in Spain there are three major *empresarios,* or managers, and they control the majority of the bullrings," Fulton says, standing in front of one of the mounted bull's heads that he has fought and killed in the arena. He rubs his fingers over the bristly hair as he continues:

"If they don't want you to perform, you don't, no matter how talented or willing you are. To have an American matador on the program that day in Jerez would have been particularly appropriate. But the ring manager shut me out. I was left with no choice. I could either tie the cowbell around my neck and forget about bullfighting, or make a gesture like jumping into the ring and fighting a bull. I felt I had to do it.

"I choreographed the whole thing," he continues, "practiced for two days in an empty ring, then went to the Jerez arena and scouted out the seat where I wanted to sit. I had it worked out to where it would take a maximum of five seconds to get from my seat and jump into the ring. I even wore a double-breasted blazer with a telescoping camera tripod inside so all I had to do was open it up and make the coat into a small *muleta,* the red cape."

Fulton made one mistake. He had counted on the fact that everyone in the ring would be so shocked to see him there, a full matador (novice fighters occasionally jump into the ring to gain attention), that they would hesitate before doing anything. Fulton would make a few passes with his coat, the crowd would cheer, and the protest statement would be made. However, when Fulton jumped into the ring one of the *banderilleros* (bullfighter's helpers) cut him off halfway to the bull and tore the jacket from the American's grasp. There was no way to fight the bull.

"I should have used the bull that El Cordobés was fighting that day," Fulton sighs. "Afterward he told me, 'If you had jumped in on my bull, I would have given you *my muleta!*'"

He pauses, looking at a photograph on the wall, his favorite, which shows him passing a deadly Miura bull with the *muleta,* disdainfully "counting the house" as the bull charges past. "Here I was, a *full matador* at the height of my career, and I couldn't get a fight!"

John Fulton is the first and only American to be promoted in Spain to bullfighting's highest professional rank, *Matador de Toros,* and have that status confirmed in Madrid. He has appeared in the world's most important bullrings, "cutting" awards with the top Spanish and Mexican matadors of the 1960s and 1970s: Ordoñez, El Cordobés, Diego Puerta,

Luis Procuna—but it has not been easy. Spanish bullfighting *aficionados* were reluctant to accept the American as a matador. Even though he was brave and competent in the bullring, he did not have—as the Spanish say—the *sangre,* the blood, of a Spanish matador. Managers looked with scorn upon his efforts. "Who wants to see a baseball player in a matador's suit," they would say, and wave him away.

Once the bullring manager in Seville sent Fulton into the ring to fight a deadly six-year-old Miura bull that the Spanish matadors had refused to fight. In this "do or die" situation, Fulton fought the bull ("a veritable cathedral," a news critic wrote), dominated it, killed well, and was awarded the bull's ear and a standing ovation from the crowd. Viewing the fight, the old master of bullfighting, Juan Belmonte, said, "Fulton fights more like a boy from Seville than from Philadelphia."

Hanging from the walls of Fulton's home are shaggy black heads of several of the bulls he has fought and killed in the ring; stuffed, mounted, yet fearsome. The heads are immense, the white horns sharp and frightening. What would it be like to stand before an animal that has been bred to kill in the ring, hear its labored breathing, smell the blood, look into its fierce eyes, see the glint of the sharp horn in the sunlight?

How would it *feel* to fight a bull . . . ?

"It's fun," Fulton says, rising from the sofa and standing, arms folded, under one of the mounted bull's heads. "In the ring I'm aware of the *sound* the bull makes, the way he *smells,* the way it feels to have him thundering past, hooves throwing sand in front of him. I can see the sand bouncing off the hard silk of my cape and hear the rattling of the sticks, the *banderillas,* as the bull goes under the red *muleta*. It is unique. Few people have sensed it."

And fear?

He pauses for a moment before answering. "A bullfighter must be terribly . . . concerned or frightened," he says finally, then shrugs. "Call it fear if you want. When the bull first comes out of what the Spanish call the Gates of Fear, and into the arena, that is the worst moment for me. It's . . . it's pretty terrifying." He pauses as if he is reluctant to admit being afraid. "I never look at the bull at that moment. I never watch him as he emerges from the black tunnel and into the light of the ring. I never watch him . . . no."

Because of the danger, matadors are superstitious. Fulton always carried a tiny bronze sculpture of a bull with him into the arena. He would rub his thumb over the metal horns for luck. Then one day he forgot it. "I realized I didn't have it," Fulton remembers, "and I thought, Oh, hell! I forgot my bull! But I went on without it. It wasn't bad luck not having it. It's only bad luck if the bull happens to toss you.

"Belmonte used to get tossed all over the ring," he continues. "There's an old saying, 'No one gets out of this business without knowing they've been there.' I've been lucky. I haven't been seriously gored. Once I was knocked silly by a bull that leapt straight up into the air as I went in with the sword for the kill." Fulton points his finger to his chin. "The horn split the front of my chin." He draws the finger under his jaw and jabs at the soft flesh. "Had the horn hit an inch further back, it would have spiked through my head."

Had he been a smaller man, the American bullfighter would have been dead.

John Fulton is a big guy for a matador. At six-one he stands much taller than his Spanish compatriots. His build is athletic and his rough-hewn profile looks amazingly like his idol, Harper Lee, the first American *Matador de Toros*. A 1910 photograph of Harper Lee hangs in Fulton's living room.

Books on bullfighting and published works by Fulton (he has been very successful writing and illustrating children's books) crowd a wall of bookcases. Off an open foyer is an Arabian lounge done in the Alhambra style with filigreed hanging lamps that cast a thousand shadows. Fulton designed the room as well as his matching Moorish bathroom. He is as proud of this exotically tiled room as he is of the sunlit studio on the second floor—where he paints in bull's blood.

"When you say bull's blood some people want to go somewhere and throw up," Fulton says with distaste. "They visualize a canvas dripping with red gore. That's not so." He holds up a painting of a bull's head. The animal is painted in swirling strokes, the muted rust tones in stark contrast to the white background.

Fulton's paintings are not of bullring scenes or fights. "They are only the image of the bulls," he says, then explains that many ancient civilizations believed the bull's life force, its soul, was contained in the blood. Fulton says he is "recreating that soul." It's commercial, of course, and the paintings sell quite well in his studio in the barrio section of Seville. A bullfighter who paints is quite unique; to paint with bull's blood is an oddity. "I know," Fulton sighs. "It's almost too bizarre."

Fulton holds the canvas at arm's length, studying it. "I feel the justification of using something as exotic as bull's blood to paint with is that you must risk your own life to get it. The only pigment I use in my paintings of bulls comes from the animals I have fought and killed in the arena." He grins, a wide-eyed boyish grin. "Of course, there is one difficulty in painting this way—you must first become a matador to get the blood.

"A bullfighter, who has to depend a great deal on agility and athletic ability, will deteriorate with age," Fulton says, then philosophizes a bit by adding, "Art, which is more permanent, can only improve with practice."

Fulton, who is now in his early sixties, realizes there are few active, old matadors. True, Belmonte fought into his late forties, as did Benvenido, who was killed in 1976 by a calf. El Gallo kept going past fifty (and a matador named Bernardo Gavino was killed at the age of seventy-four while practicing his profession), but most bullfighters quit while they are still quick enough to evade the horns.

Over the past twenty-five years Fulton has seriously considered "cutting the pigtail" and retiring from the ring. Yet, he can't force himself to do it. He occasionally fights in Mexican resort towns such as Cancún. Why continue? The adulation of the crowd? The magic of the moment in the ring? Yes, of course, but then add one more; superstardom was too close—and he feels he just missed it.

•

Fulton had become excited about bullfighting at the age of thirteen when he saw the movie *Blood and Sand* with Tyrone Power and Rita Hayworth. "I was at an impossible age," Fulton recalls, "and it seemed to me that bullfighting was the most exciting and fascinating thing anyone could do."

Learning to become a bullfighter was not as easy as trying out for the high school football team. At that time there had been little written on the subject in English; Hemingway's *Death in the Afternoon* (1927) was the notable exception. Fulton had met some Spaniards in Philadelphia, his home town. One was a barber who had been a *novillero,* an apprentice bullfighter. "I used go there to get my haircut," Fulton remembers. "The barber gave me my first bullfighting lesson with his barber's cape.

"Then I read an article by Barnaby Conrad, 'The Day I Fought with Juan Belmonte,'" Fulton says. "It seemed incredible that someone by the name of Barnaby Conrad fought bulls. But I figured another matador, Sydney Franklin, sounded just as incredible and John Fulton even more so. I wrote a letter to Conrad."

Barnaby Conrad had fought in the ring—billed as *Niño de California*—with the legendary matador, Juan Belmonte. Conrad—who had witnessed the frustration of novice bullfighters, and had written, "The operators behind the scenes of the tinsel spectacle make Machiavelli look like Little Lord Fauntleroy"—tried to dissuade Fulton from fighting bulls.

"He was very discouraging," Fulton remembers, "and told me to read the novel, *Wounds of Hunger,* which tells of the pitfalls that lie behind the glamour of the arena. But the idea of becoming a full matador was in my blood. I had to try it."

An aspiring artist, Fulton went to Mexico City on a scholarship. While there he studied bullfighting and even fought in a few small towns. He killed his first bull in 1953 when he made his debut in a *traje de luces,* the bullfighter's suit of lights, that the famous Mexican matador, Luis Procuna, had given him. "Procuna was extremely superstitious," Fulton says, "and he had had a bad afternoon with the suit, so he gave it to me. It was a little small, but I fought well in it. It wasn't bad luck for me."

Fulton continued to fight in the border towns and began to feel that he was good enough to become a matador. But there were too many American novices fighting bulls in Mexico. It was difficult to be taken seriously, so he decided to go to Spain, become a matador, get the "Spanish Good Housekeeping Seal of Approval," then return to Mexico in triumph. The place to achieve his goals was Seville; the cradle of bullfighting, the classic city of *Carmen,* Cervantes—and the deadly Miura bulls.

Fulton bought a one-way ticket to Spain. He had a few hundred dollars in his pocket and a letter of introduction from Barnaby Conrad. "Conrad's letter was not really an introduction," Fulton admits. "He had written me and said where I could find the great matador Juan Belmonte—at a café at such-and-such a time. 'Tell him you're a friend of mine and the rest is up to you,' was all Conrad said. And that's what I did. Belmonte was sitting in the restaurant and I went up to him and introduced myself as an American matador."

Just like that. To Don Juan Belmonte, the most famous matador of his time, "The Earthquake from Triana," the greatest bullfighter of the century. And Belmonte looked at the tall American, saw the desire in his eyes, and said, "Someday you must come to my ranch." And Fulton replied, "Whatever you say."

Months later Belmonte contacted Fulton and told him to come to the ranch for a *tienta,* where they test calves in the ring for bravery. Belmonte added, "Bring along a cape."

It was a decisive moment in Fulton's bullfighting career. He was broke and completely demoralized. Almost convinced that he didn't have what it took to be a matador, the American planned on asking Belmonte his opinion. If the great matador thought he had a chance of becoming even a mediocre bullfighter, then Fulton would stick it out. If Belmonte hedged and said something like, "This is a very difficult profession," Fulton would be on the next freighter home.

At the ranch Belmonte turned to his American guest and told him to go into the ring and fight one of the bull calves. Perspiring from nervousness, Fulton fought the young animal, then when he went over the horns for a symbolic kill, he realized everyone on the veranda was standing and applauding, including the *maestro* himself. Belmonte wrapped his arms around Fulton and said to the other guests, "If I had seen John fight and did not know his name, there would be no way of telling he was not Spanish. He is the best non-Latin bullfighter I have seen."

That was enough for Fulton. He was determined to become a bullfighter.

But even with Belmonte's recommendation he was still a *gringo*. The *empresarios* of the big rings closed the Gates of Fear to him. He *was* getting a few fights in small-town fiestas, but it was slow progress. In the old, but classic, ring in Puerto de Santa Maria, he had several successful fights and was afterward triumphantly carried through the streets on the shoulders of admirers.

But it wasn't working. He had to fight in Seville or Madrid to get recognition. "I was banging my head against the *barrera* trying to get in Seville. The *empresario* kept saying he would put me on the *cartel,* the program, *if* I was still around, which in Spain is the same as saying, 'If you don't get killed.' The Madrid manager said he would give me a fight *after* I had fought in Seville. It was a real run-around."

Then suddenly, Fulton got a call from Madrid offering a fight the following Sunday. Snap! Just like that. He would be making his debut as a *novillero* in the biggest ring in Spain. He was ecstatic—but worried.

He had fought only once that year. He was rusty. He borrowed money and bought a bull to practice on. The animal turned out to be blind and worthless. That was on Wednesday. Four more days to go. He *had* to find another animal to practice on.

Then that afternoon he got a call offering him a fight in the Puerto de Santa Maria ring substituting for a *novillero* who had been gored. "Two bulls," Fulton thought, "and a good public in a ring where I'm known. Of course I'll fight. But what if something happens; what if I get gored. I'll miss Madrid." But he needed the practice so he took the chance.

It was a terrible mistake.

That Thursday the second bull tossed the young American, barely missing his body with a horn, but tore an ugly gash in the bullfighter's foot. Fulton limped around and finished killing the bull, but that night the foot was swollen like a balloon. Madrid was only two days away.

Hobbled with pain, Fulton went into the Madrid ring that Sunday knowing he had to fight, or never be asked to fight again.

Everything went wrong.

Fulton could barely move around the arena. His footwork was horrible; no grace or beauty. The bulls were huge—the first one weighed 500 kilos—far too big for a *novillero* fight. Fulton's second bull was a large, long-legged animal with sweeping horns, and looked more like a gray mule than a bull. The crowd roared with laughter. They were out to razz the misplaced *norteamericano*. They weren't there for his debut, but for his funeral.

When the "moment of truth" came, Fulton went in with the sword to kill the ungainly animal, but the sword went only halfway in. Fulton describes the fiasco:

"Somehow the sword worked out, and since the bull hadn't been weakened properly with the *picador's* lances, the bull seemed to grow in strength. It kept getting more wary and more treacherous because it knew what was happening. It was going to 'school' and I was the teacher."

Fulton pauses, the line of his mouth grim. "I wasn't able to kill the bull in the time limit. It was taken out of the ring alive. (The bull is immediately slaughtered for meat.) It was the only time in my career that I was unable to kill the bull."

The Spanish *aficionados* have a saying, *El único que no tiene verguenza es el toro*—The only one that doesn't have any shame is the bull. Fulton felt the shame. He felt foolish and was so embarrassed he didn't think he could go out on the street again.

The bullfight critics blasted him in brutal reviews: "Señor Fulton has proved once again that a *norteamericano* has no business in a bullfight, and they should be barred from the arena by law!" Author Barnaby Conrad later commented: "Anyone with less guts and determination than John would have slunk back to America, appeared on 'What's My Line?' then meekly taken a job in Philadelphia as a clerk."

But Fulton stayed on.

"I was pretty much a disaster at that point," Fulton remembers with a sigh. "But it was a good experience in that it was a tempering process. I began to think that it was incredible the way the Spanish critics were treating me. I was just a novice bullfighter making my debut, and they were razzing me as though I were a *figuro de toreo,* a leading matador. I said to hell with it, patched up my wounded pride, and got started again.

Miraculously, the fiasco in Madrid brought Fulton's name into the limelight. Through hard work he was able to wrangle a few *corridas* (even one in Seville)—and fought well. Then it came time to talk to Antonio Ordoñez, Spain's leading active matador.

Two years earlier Fulton had appeared in a festival fight with Ordoñez, had fought well, and was awarded two ears and a tail from the bull he fought. Ordoñez was impressed and offered to sponsor Fulton for the American's *alternativa,* the ceremony where one matador advances the apprentice into the ranks of *Matador de Toros*—a full matador!

Ordoñez had stipulated that Fulton must fight in Seville and Madrid first as a novice. This he had done, so he went to see the great matador. And that's when Ordoñez wrote the would-be American matador off by bluntly telling him, "Perhaps God hasn't chosen you for this road."

"I really felt I could have killed Antonio Ordoñez right then," Fulton recalls. His eyes burn at the thought of this rejection. "I think I would have if I'd had one ounce of gypsy blood in me. I looked him square in the eye and said, "Antonio, whether God has chosen me for this road or not, I'm going to become a *matador de toros.*"

And he did—in Seville.

The Seville bullring is over three hundred years old, and is the most respected and magnificent *Plaza de Toros* in the world. It is also the toughest; the *aficionados* the most critical; the bulls the largest. By 1963 only thirty-two men in the twentieth century had become matadors in the Seville bullring. American John Fulton was going to try and realize his dream by becoming the arena's thirty-third matador. The *alternativa* was to be given to Fulton by José Maria Montilla, a respected senior matador.

Once again it wasn't easy.

A week before the Seville *corrida* Fulton pulled a ligament in a practice fight and ended up in bed under an infrared lamp with a heating pad covering one knee. "I didn't know what to do," Fulton says. "Here I was with an opportunity of a lifetime, and I couldn't walk. It looked like Madrid all over again."

Fulton stayed in bed right up to fight time, and then put on his *traje de luces* and walked into the Seville bullring to become a matador.

He was a little tentative on his first bull, favoring the bad leg, but soon the adrenaline began flowing, the pain subsided, and he began to give the bull fine classic passes which forced reluctant shouts of *Olé!* from the crowd. The audience, who had come to jeer the American out of the ring, was impressed enough after the kill to applaud until Fulton took a lap around the ring to acknowledge the tribute.

Then it was time for Fulton's second bull.

It was a monster, a six-year-old animal that weighed 600 kilos. The bull was like the legendary ones that Joselito and Belmonte fought forty years before in the golden age of bullfighting. The crowd of *aficionados* knew the American wouldn't be able to handle it. But Fulton was determined to fight well. And he mastered the bull, moving gracefully with the cape before the huge animal's charges. And he heard for the first time an arena of thirteen thousand people chanting, *Olé, Olé! OLÉ!* with each pass. And then it was over.

He killed the bull with a well-placed sword thrust and as he stepped into the center of the ring to listen to the applause of the crowd, the thought pounded in his head—"I am a matador—A MATADOR!"

Then, on October 12, 1967, fifteen years after his first fight, and four years after taking his *alternativa* in Seville, John Fulton confirmed his status as a matador in Madrid. He had accomplished what no other American had done—but he was through. Rather than opening doors, it snapped on the final lock and bolt. Why? Perhaps the Spanish were embarrassed to have an American matador excel at what only a Spaniard was supposed to do well. Perhaps he had become too good. Perhaps . . .

"I know I'm never going to get a shot at the big money, and I'm too far along the line at my age to think that the Spanish will say, 'Hey, you really are a good bullfighter.'" Fulton looks at the framed profile of his idol, Harper Lee, then continues in an even voice. "But . . . I am a matador.

"And I will die a matador."